Offshore

ALSO BY BROOKE HARRINGTON

Capital Without Borders: Wealth Managers and the One Percent

Deception: From Ancient Empires to Internet Dating

Pop Finance: Investment Clubs and the New Investor Populism

NORTON
SHORTS

Offshore

Stealth Wealth and the New Colonialism

BROOKE HARRINGTON

W. W. NORTON & COMPANY
Independent Publishers Since 1923

For information about permission to reproduce selections from
this book, write to Permissions, W. W. Norton & Company, Inc.,
500 Fifth Avenue, New York, NY 10110

For information about special discounts for bulk purchases, please
contact W. W. Norton Special Sales at specialsales@wwnorton.com
or 800-233-4830

Manufacturing by Lakeside Harrisonburg
Production manager: Delaney Adams

ISBN: 978-1-324-06494-7

W. W. Norton & Company, Inc.
500 Fifth Avenue, New York, N.Y. 10110
www.wwnorton.com

W. W. Norton & Company Ltd.
15 Carlisle Street, London W1D 3BS

10 9 8 7 6 5 4 3 2 1

For Kristen

CONTENTS

Offshore

INTRODUCTION

"Why do you study offshore finance?"

I get this question a lot. Usually, I explain how fascinating it is to research a topic in which so many social forces intersect, from economics and politics to families and culture. The real answer is much briefer: destiny.

F. Scott Fitzgerald once called my hometown "the most glamorous place in the world." On the shores of Lake Michigan about an hour north of Chicago, Lake Forest inspired Fitzgerald's *The Great Gatsby* and provided the setting for Robert Redford's Oscar-winning film *Ordinary People*: two haunting meditations on wealth and secrets. When people ask me how I came to build a career around studying a system that shrouds great fortunes in secrecy, I can say—like Hamlet—that "I am native here, and to the manner born."

Throughout my upbringing, my schoolmates had the wealth while I had the secrets. I sat in public elementary school next to the scions of midwestern royalty: the descendants of the Armours and the Swifts, who built the meatpacking industry that Upton Sinclair exposed, along with the daughters of media and banking barons, whose lakefront mansions resembled the settings of Tom and Daisy Buchanan's raucous parties. Meanwhile, on the wrong side of town, where Lake Forest peters out into prairie and we could hear (and smell) cows being milked at five each evening, I made dinner for my family: my mother, who worked in downtown Chicago and came back late; my little sister, so disabled by spina bifida and hydrocephalus that she never learned to walk or talk; and occasionally my father, a would-be Gatsby whose fatal flaws eventually landed him in jail. One of our biggest secrets was that we were on public assistance, or "welfare" as my mother called it, because my sister's medical bills had mounted to over a million dollars, equivalent to about $6 million today—an almost unimaginable sum for a middle-class family in the mid-1970s.

The only time I ever got in trouble at school was in the third grade, after a classmate asked whether I had siblings. I naïvely told the whole truth, including that my sister went to a special school for disabled children. The classmate called her a "retard," and I experienced a new emotion: fury driven by protectiveness. I decked that kid. It was the first and only time I punched someone, and the end of my social life as a grade-schooler. Disability and knuckle sandwiches were not *comme il faut* in the finer homes of Lake Forest. It was a lasting lesson about cultivating discretion and invisibility for self-protection.

When my sister died, a few months later, I had to keep it to myself and power through as if nothing had happened. I couldn't stay home, because my mom couldn't afford to miss work, and my dad had run off to Mexico for a couple of years. There was nowhere else to go but Mrs. Lockwood's classroom, the calmest and safest place in my life. My place of refuge was also my joy, so I built a future among teachers and books.

When I was still in middle school, *The Official Preppy Handbook* came out and I studied it like an anthropologist, trying to learn the customs and rituals of a people with whom I could only be an observer. Like Fitzgerald, I could see that the rich were different—and, like him, I wanted to understand why. Decades later, when I became a professional sociologist, participant observation was the method I used to crack open the world of offshore finance and the elite fortunes it held. In a setting so fiercely guarded against outsiders, the only way to investigate this world was to join it. The ultra-wealthy and the professionals who serve them don't otherwise talk with nosy sociologists.

My goal was to make sense of the economic and political inequality spiraling out of control worldwide, so I went to the "engine room" driving the whole phenomenon. When I began studying offshore finance in 2007, I'd already been an economic sociology professor for nearly a decade, and I'd "warmed up" for this new project by publishing books on the sociology of investing in America (*Pop Finance*), as well as on the secrecy and lies surrounding wealth (*Deception: From Ancient Empires to Internet Dating*). But I knew something was missing: offshore finance loomed like a black hole at the periphery of both studies, exerting an influence that was palpable but for which sociological theory and concepts were still lacking.

In my own research as well as in the news, all signs pointed to an urgent need for more study of the uppermost reaches of the socioeconomic spectrum. This territory had been all but abandoned by sociologists since the 1970s, partly for political reasons (such as expressing solidarity with and advocacy for the poor) and partly for reasons of data availability. The wealthier people are, the more difficult they are to study. In contrast, data on the poor and the middle-class have always been much easier to access. As the wealthy retreated behind gated communities or onto private islands, and secured financial-legal expertise to shroud their fortunes in secrecy, it became prohibitively costly—in terms of time as well as money—to study them.

Having grown up among the ultra-rich, I was undeterred. That's because I knew something most people don't: the wealthy don't manage their own money. Many, like the parents of the chewing-gum heiress I met at summer camp, didn't even know how to change their own light bulbs. They had housekeepers and other "staff" to handle the daily challenges the rest of us face ourselves. Do-it-yourself financial management was out of the question for most of them—particularly because their fortunes were multigenerational, usually transnational, and far too complex for any one person to grow and protect. To develop any real understanding of how the rich were getting richer, I would have to talk with the cadre of professionals—the trustees, private bankers, tax advisers, and other members of the wealth management team—that virtually all rich families employ.

The problem was, how to gain access to those professionals? I couldn't just call or email to request interviews, because in many jurisdictions, the experts face significant legal penalties for sharing secrets about their practices—including fines and even prison time. They were the best point of access to all I wanted to understand, but they might as well have been standing on the other side of an alligator-filled moat. Even if I could reach them, how could I persuade them to tell me anything of value?

Lots of other social scientists are interested in offshore finance—economists, geographers, and political scientists, to name a few—but they generally haven't tried to leap the alligator-filled moat and engage with the people who make the offshore system function. They mostly rely on information from sources such as surveys, transaction records, or historical archives. These sources have significant limitations. Ultimately, to study secrets—particularly those connected to hidden fortunes—you have to roll up your sleeves and engage with human beings.

This perspective was articulated most eloquently and memorably by the mid-twentieth-century sociologist C. Wright Mills. Colorful, outlandish, an *enfant terrible* of sorts, Mills taught at Columbia University from 1946 until his untimely death in 1962. We still use phrases he coined, such as "the power elite"—which became the title of one of his most famous books. Mills was interested in inequality, and particularly in the people at the top of the socioeconomic ladder, so his views are relevant to my own work on offshore finance, which explores how contemporary power elites conceal the wealth that maintains their influence over world affairs.

Mills is also remembered for his distinctive method of sociological research, a hybrid of biography and scientific inquiry. The most interesting discoveries, he argued, come from reflecting on our personal experiences as parts of larger social systems. To make sense of the world in any new or interesting way requires us to link the personal to the world-historical, and the biographical to the structural. Mills called this the "sociological imagination": a connection-making process in which "the human meaning of public issues must be revealed by relating them to personal troubles—and to the problems of individual life."

Inspired by Mills's vision, I decided not only to write about offshore finance but to write about it in a new way—as if I were the biographer of a very complex, interesting, powerful, and dangerous person. This method would help overcome the biggest challenge for anyone trying to explain offshore finance: the difficulty of making complicated legal and financial affairs interesting to nonspecialists. Even those who *do* specialize in this system sometimes use the term MEGO (My Eyes Glazeth Over) to describe it.

My objective in this book is to bring to life all the things that make offshore finance compelling, surprising, contradictory, and occasionally frightening. I want to show you that offshore is immensely significant and worthy of your attention, even if—maybe especially if—you're not one of the ultra-wealthy people using it to hide a fortune. As part of this strategy, I'll tell you about my own encounters with the system and I'll introduce you to some of my informants, including the pin-striped London bounty hunter who collects debts from deadbeat oligarchs and the Maori fisherman who crystallized my understanding of offshore finance as a neocolonial enterprise. For those interested in greater depth on some of the subjects I'll touch on, I've included at the end of this book pointers to the readings that have most enriched my own understanding: works by historians, economists, anthropologists, political scientists, and journalists. As you'll see, there is far more to be said about offshore finance than could ever fit into this slim volume.

But back to the alligator-filled moat. How to cross it and, once I did, how to get useful information? It was clear that I could not approach this as a conventional piece of research, because of the secrecy surrounding offshore practices. Nor could I use deception to gather data—for example, by posing as a wealthy potential client for offshore financial services. The ethics rules of twenty-first-century sociology require researchers to disclose their real identities and their reasons for conducting a study. Had I failed to do so, my work would have been excluded from research funding—a major issue, since it cost about $400,000 to gather data over a decade—and my work could not have been accepted for publication in scholarly outlets.

Such constraints have likely played a major role in precluding other researchers from studying offshore finance. I was able to surmount the barriers only by making a risky move: I joined the secret-keepers club by training to become an offshore wealth manager.

The method I used is called "immersion ethnography." While it's uncommon these days due to the high costs in time, effort, and money, it is among the very oldest of old-school approaches to social science. In fact, its roots stretch back to the turn of the last century, when anthropologists and sociologists sought to understand the world primarily by observing and living among the people who interested them. In contemporary practice, it is often used as a technique of last resort when faced with a group too secretive or defensive to permit exploration. Recently, a few well-known studies have used immersion ethnography to study drug dealers, criminals, and the people who inhabit the VIP rooms of exclusive nightclubs. Turning this technique on a professional group at work, however, is very rare.

Fortunately for me, someone else had blazed that trail: John Van Maanen, now an emeritus professor at MIT. As a young PhD student in the late 1960s in Southern California, Van Maanen wanted to observe police officers for his dissertation research. But they weren't keen on being observed, given the extreme tension and distrust that had arisen between them and the public following the Watts Uprising of 1965: a conflict comparable in its national impact to George Floyd's murder in 2020. After getting nowhere with polite inquiries—more than a dozen of his written requests to study area police were rejected—Van Maanen got creative. He enrolled in the police academy and underwent the full training process to become a police officer, including going out on armed patrols. Only then did he build enough trust and cooperation with his fellow officers to conduct his research.

By embracing the idea that ethnography lends itself to biographical reflection, Van Maanen exemplified everything that Mills had outlined years before. He showed that sociologists can reveal the most about a phenomenon when they enter into it, then analyze and integrate their own experiences. That strategy, when applied to groups that resist transparency but wield significant power, proved transformative for my own work.

Formally, the people I studied were called wealth managers, but they could more accurately have been described as secrecy experts. While Van Maanen's training program lasted a few months, mine lasted two years. I could invest this time only thanks to a research fellowship I was awarded in Germany, which freed me from teaching and administrative responsibilities for that period. While there, I pieced together a patchwork of funding to cover the $50,000 tuition fee for the wealth management training program. The program's curriculum consisted of five separate classes, each of which involved months of at-home preparation by reading through a huge course packet—hundreds of pages in giant binders the size of major metropolitan phone books. For each subject, this at-home study was followed by a week-long in-person class, involving four days of nine-to-five instruction, culminating in a four-hour written exam on day five. Overall, this part of the project required two solid years of surprisingly intense study and thousands of miles of travel to the various course venues. While I never got a job or even moonlighted as a wealth manager, earning that credential opened doors to a secretive realm that would otherwise have remained closed to me.

That is how I came to spend many hours in dismal airport hotels and conference centers in otherwise lovely settings like Switzerland and the Cayman Islands, learning about trust and corporate law, financial investment, and accounting. The courses on trust and corporate law were challenging in a fun way; the courses on finance and accounting, not so much. But that investment of time and effort made everything else possible. The process not only served to familiarize me with the field and its practices but—most importantly—put me face-to-face with experts who would never ordinarily have spoken to me. The classes were full of experienced practitioners, not the trainees I expected. Because wealth management had started to define itself as a distinct profession only in the early 1990s, there was no globally recognized credential for practitioners until almost a decade later. Prior to that, attorneys, accountants, bankers, and others would just specialize—both intentionally and by happenstance—in serving the ultra-rich. When a globally recognized professional certification process emerged in the early 2000s, many clients and employers soon came to expect it. The credential, established by the international professional society for wealth managers (the London-based Society of Trust and Estate Practitioners), rapidly became a required qualification for wealth management jobs advertised in the *Financial Times* and other industry publications.

This new requirement led many experienced practitioners from all over the world to enroll in the training courses I was taking, even though many of them had already worked for years, even decades, in wealth management. They were mostly attorneys by training, or accountants, but there was also a smattering of bankers and even the occasional ex-academic. The courses were taught by highly experienced wealth managers, several of whom had authored the textbooks we were using in class.

Between the classes and the coffee and lunch breaks, I spent about two hundred hours with these practitioners. Because we generally stayed in the conference hotels where the courses were held, opportunities for informal interaction were abundant, allowing me to buttonhole my new colleagues for interviews or just to observe them sharing war stories and professional gossip. The credential I earned after two years was my entry ticket to professional meetings for wealth managers— gatherings where thousands of practitioners met to share best practices and innovations, where I could also observe and recruit participants for my study.

I did not go undercover. Throughout the research process, I disclosed my real name, institutional affiliation, and research aims, per the requirements of modern sociological research ethics. Whether I was attending classes or professional society meetings, I always wore a name tag that included my place of work, so it was clear that I was a scholar affiliated with a research institution. When I started, I didn't know if anyone would talk with me. Somewhat to my surprise, the majority of practitioners I met were quite willing to talk, with my assurance of anonymity. As German sociologist Georg Simmel pointed out at the turn of the last century, something about meeting a stranger makes many people wish to unburden themselves. In consequence, he wrote, the stranger "often receives the most surprising openness."

Wealth managers' openness with me may have been driven by the paradoxical way in which my presence was unthreatening in some respects but provocative in others. Fieldwork, as Van Maanen wrote, is always "both a social and a personal act." That means the data gathered are inextricable from the personal characteristics of the researcher eliciting and collecting them. As nearly a century of research on social psychology has shown, looking or acting "too different" within a group arouses distrust and suspicion, making people unwilling to talk. Researchers must look similar enough to the people they study to be trusted, at least provisionally and for the length of a conversation. Van Maanen blended well with his research setting: he was a young white man among other young or middle-aged white men. He even wore the same kind of clothes as off-duty officers, right down to the clip-on ties. These characteristics, he wrote, didn't fully make him "one of the boys" but, rather, situated him as an "acceptable incompetent": someone who knew enough to keep up with the professionals but was understood to be in need of many patient explanations.

In some respects, I was also viewed as an "acceptable incompetent." Though I blended in as a white, able-bodied, native-English-speaking professional, I also stood out by virtue of being a woman within the male-dominated offshore world. Women still make up a minority of finance professionals; that can lead to being underestimated and undermined.

In the labor force, those obstacles can cost a bundle in lost earnings. But in the world of ethnography, being treated as a dummy can be a gift. When you're seen as harmless and bumbling, out of your depth, you're not perceived as a threat. You might call this "the Columbo effect," after the 1970s TV detective whose slightly confused and rumpled demeanor always inspired the bad guys to spill the beans. In the presence of an acceptable incompetent, many people let down their guard and volunteer very revealing information.

My mere presence as a woman in a place so overwhelmingly populated by male attorneys, bankers, and other financial experts was read as an invitation for them to hold forth and explain things to me. This effect was accentuated while I was heavily pregnant, like an offshore version of Marge Gunderson, the police chief in the movie *Fargo*. Often, my biggest problem was writing notes quickly enough to keep up with the volume of data coming my way. One of my best informants—an elegant German wealth manager who had just retired after an illustrious forty-year career—was so excited to share his "war stories" that he only stopped talking, after three and a half hours, because the waitstaff at the café where we were sitting had started putting the chairs atop the tables and sweeping up around us.

As with Columbo, there was sometimes an element of the confessional about these interactions. Virtually all the wealth managers I spoke with felt—like the police officers after Watts in Van Maanen's study—that their profession was deeply misunderstood and unfairly maligned. Some may have seen me as a means to set the record straight. Others were conscience-stricken about the impact their work was having on the growing economic and political inequality in the world. Though it would have been risky for them to share those struggles with their co-workers (who could use it against them) or with family members (who might fear the loss of the wealth manager's livelihood), they could treat an interview with me as an informal confessional.

By putting me face-to-face with practicing wealth managers, and demonstrating that they *would* speak with me, those initial two years in the credential course provided the proof of concept I needed in order to get research funding and take the project further. For the next six years, I traveled to every region of the world, from glossy European and North American capitals, to developing countries in South America and Africa, to islands in the Indian Ocean, the Caribbean, and the South Pacific. The credential opened doors firmly closed to the public, allowing me to join wealth managers at professional society meetings and observe them in their offices.

Since then, the offshore system has kept changing and revealing itself in ways that have surprised me. In September 2015, when I submitted to the publisher my first book on offshore finance (*Capital Without Borders*), the Panama Papers leak hadn't yet become public. But six months later, all those offshore skeletons—11.5 million documents from the Panama City wealth management firm Mossack Fonseca—came tumbling out and changed everything. With the two major offshore leaks that followed, the Paradise Papers of 2017 and the Pandora Papers of 2021, the world learned of financial corruption on an almost unimaginable scale. It would have seemed like a conspiracy theory if the records hadn't been laid bare for all to see. Later revelations concerning the role of offshore finance in 2016 electoral politics on both sides of the Atlantic, as well as in the 2022 invasion of Ukraine, have underscored how influential this secretive system remains. What in the early 2000s had looked like an esoteric research topic—one that seemed arcane even to my most supportive colleagues in economic sociology—kept bursting into relevance.

As of this writing, I've interviewed seventy wealth managers in nineteen countries, and I plan to keep gathering data as long as I can. Every month, sometimes more often, I learn something new about how offshore works or how it affects everyday life far beyond the world of the super-rich. Now, at year sixteen of this research, with no end in sight, it looks like Van Maanen was prophetic when he told me, just nine months after I started, that this would be a "lifetime project."

It all began with learning in childhood that secret about the very rich: their dependence on hired help at all levels. That was the key that allowed me to enter new research territory. But investigating the secrets and legalized lawlessness of some global elites required skills that don't appear in an academic CV. Accessing their world through a servants' entrance involved creativity and resourcefulness, because nothing in the methodological training I'd received had prepared me for breaching secretive places where I wasn't welcome. I just had to figure it out as I went along and persist despite some unexpected dangers. Some of the best data I collected emerged from things going very wrong. It's one thing to know intellectually that the clients for offshore financial services are deadly serious about guarding their secrets. It's much more illuminating to confront the reality face-to-face.

CHAPTER 1

The Unauthorized Biography of a Secretive System

THE REAL SUBJECT OF THIS book is a system. While systems often seem boring and impersonal, offshore finance is the stuff of swashbuckling thrillers and tabloid gossip rags, with a cast of characters that includes celebrities and modern-day buccaneers. The 2016 Panama Papers exposed the inner workings of the system to many for the first time. It was a media sensation, revealing a web of connections involving A-listers such as the actors Jackie Chan and Emma Watson, as well as the king of Saudi Arabia and business leaders like a former CEO of Adidas. It also laid bare the ways that offshore finance corrodes our most important democratic, economic, and social institutions, spawning decay that creeps into the everyday lives of billions of people.

Despite the headline-grabbing aspects of the Panama Papers story, and the handful of leaks that followed, offshore finance has generated much less notice than it deserves—and even less resistance—simply because most people forget that it exists. Occasional reminders crop up in the news, such as the recent prosecution of the largest tax fraud in U.S. history: a scheme carried out by a software entrepreneur who stashed $2 billion in offshore accounts. But most reporting doesn't make clear that this affects the rest of us. Few realize that they're paying a lot more in taxes and bank borrowing costs because of elites' use of Cook Islands trusts or South Dakota shell companies. Nor do they know how much of the dark money that undermines democracies and fuels environmental degradation flows through offshore financial centers. As a matter of public interest, it should be widely known that offshore finance is not just about naughty celebrities and tax avoidance: it's the platform for an elite insurgency opposed to basic principles like equality before the law, economic stability, free markets, and social solidarity.

"Tax haven" is a common term in the news, but it's quite misleading about what offshore finance really is. It's a system that sells secrecy to the very rich. Shielding wealth from taxes is just one of the many by-products of that transaction.

Wealth and secrecy go hand in hand, as German sociologist Georg Simmel observed more than a century ago. The kind of inequality that endures and grows over generations, in which the rich get richer while the rest languish, thrives best when least examined. Secrets themselves can be a kind of wealth: Simmel called them "inner private property." Like gold and jewels, he wrote, some secrets adorn the possessor and signify to others "I have something which you do not have." It seems an apt metaphor: as the rest of us are more surveilled than ever before, the secrecy offshore finance provides has become a luxury status symbol as well as an invaluable tool for maintaining power.

Secrecy confers impunity: freedom from accountability, both to social norms and to the law. Offshore "secrecy havens" make it possible for some corporations, and a very small group of individuals—including many of the world's approximately three thousand billionaires—to escape constraints the rest of us take for granted. Freedom from taxation is just the beginning. That's why some economists call off-shore centers "fiscal paradise": they represent a transcendent plane of existence where many earthly rules cease to apply for a financially blessed few.

Vulnerable to lawsuits? Move your fortune to the Cook Islands, as the Rothschilds and many other wealthy families have done. The laws of that tiny archipelago—a Shangri-La located roughly between Fiji and Tahiti—won't protect your fortune from taxes, but they do create an impenetrable shield against any claims by foreign litigants. Even the U.S. government has been unable to collect assets stashed in the Cook Islands by fraudsters convicted in federal court. These include infomercial king Kevin Trudeau, the author of a series of books based on conspiracy theories, including—ironically enough—one called *Debt Cures "They" Don't Want You to Know About.* Since 2011, Trudeau has owed Uncle Sam $37.6 million. Thanks to the effective workings of the offshore financial system, the most economically and politically pow-erful government in the world has been unable to collect one red cent of that federal court judgment.

But offshore can do so much more! Anticipating a costly divorce? No problem—just stash your assets in an offshore trust. Legally, they are no longer yours and can't be attached in a judgment. Consider the case of the Russian billionaire Dmitry Rybolovlev, who a few years back settled what was called "the most expensive divorce in history." Although a Swiss court initially awarded half of Rybolovlev's roughly $9 billion fortune to his ex-wife, Elena, an appeals court later ruled that most of those assets were untouchable in the divorce settlement because they were held in trust.

Don't want to abide by campaign finance laws or environmental regulations? Compliance with those rules costs money and limits influence. But offshore corporations, foundations, and trusts can provide workarounds. For example, the destruction of the Amazon rainforest—often termed "the lungs of the world"—has been financed in recent years by offshore accounts that shrouded the projects in secrecy, allowing their backers to evade the regulatory and media scrutiny that might have stopped them. The former president of Chile was recently exposed for using offshore finance not only to conceal the bribes he received and evade his own country's taxes but to hide one other source of his personal wealth: the profit he made from an illegal mining operation that threatens 80 percent of the world's Humboldt penguin population.

According to the Financial Action Task Force, an international watchdog group, environmental crime is among the most lucrative in the world: as of 2021, it was estimated to net criminals between $110 and $280 billion annually. But all those profits would be as worthless as Monopoly money without the offshore financial system. Before the billions can be spent on luxury villas and superyachts, they must first be laundered into the legitimate financial system. That's where offshore financial centers and their "light regulatory regimes" become indispensable. If you or I make a big deposit to an onshore bank, perhaps as a down payment on a house, we'll be required to document the origin of those funds; if we don't have the kind of salary that could justify a $2 million savings account, the bank won't do business with us. But offshore, the rule for big deposits is often "don't ask, don't tell." Once you put the money in a shell company or a trust in places like Cyprus or Nevis—where you won't be asked pesky questions about your illegal fishing or logging activities—those structures can funnel cash into respectable banks and businesses in London or New York. From there, the funds appear "clean" and you can use them as you wish.

Ironically, the offshore financial centers facilitating these crimes are often among the most vulnerable places in the world to climate change. Singapore, an island city known as the "Switzerland of Asia" for its booming offshore business, launched a new research center in 2023 to combat what the government called the "existential threat" posed by rising sea levels. Some of that environmental threat has been created by the financial services industry itself. This is also the case in the Cayman Islands, which are rapidly losing their critically important wetlands ecosystem to the offshore business community's demands for more land on which to construct their office buildings. The Caymans' wetland mangrove trees literally hold the country together, preventing hurricanes from obliterating the islands. At the current pace of development, the mangroves are expected to disappear by 2108.

From these examples, and from evocative terms like "fiscal paradise," you might get the impression that offshore finance happens exclusively on palm-fringed islands. But that's not the case at all. Offshore financial centers are jurisdictions (countries, states, or city-states, like Singapore) that use their laws mainly to attract foreign capital—not so much from investors but, rather, from wealthy individuals and multinational firms seeking escape from *other* countries' laws. This means offshore centers keep their regulations, as well as taxes, to the barest minimum. By far their most important offering is secrecy, via laws that conceal the identities and assets of corporate and individual clients. It is thus impossible to know exactly how many people and firms make use of the offshore financial system, or exactly how much money is out there. UC Berkeley economist Gabriel Zucman and his colleagues estimate that, as of the end of 2022, at least $12 trillion in private household wealth is hidden offshore—roughly 12 percent of all the wealth produced in the world that year. The mammoth size of these capital flows and the integration of offshore financial strategies into everyday corporate activity (most U.S. pension funds and corporate bonds rely on offshore companies) mean that the offshore financial system isn't remote or arcane at all: it's a central feature of the world economy.

You don't have to go far to find an offshore secrecy haven. In fact, a couple of the world's most popular offshore centers are on U.S. soil. Those of us who live here just call them states. Delaware is arguably the best-known corporate tax haven on the planet, and many wealthy individuals—provided they are not U.S. citizens—choose South Dakota, Wyoming, and Nevada to cache their assets. For many high-net-worth individuals, the United States has eclipsed Switzerland as the capital of secrecy and security.

As these examples suggest, the term "offshore" can be misleading. Any place, including landlocked Switzerland or Wyoming, can be an offshore financial center for someone. While some of those places do resemble the fiscal paradises of popular imagination, describing all the countries in the system as "offshore" is just an historical holdover from the era of maritime trade. During the Age of Exploration, when most goods could be transported internationally only via ships, sixteenth-century traders created special economic zones known as "free ports." There, the usual restrictions on commerce did not apply—including which nationalities could exchange goods and what taxes would be levied on the transactions. International travelers still enjoy this innovation in the form of duty-free stores at airports and cruise ship harbors.

Creating areas outside the normal rule of law became vitally important to the expansion of colonial empires in the seventeenth century, as imperialism came into conflict with mercantilism. Closed commercial systems ring-fenced by protectionist policies—such as the rule that English colonies could trade only with English ships—put a damper on profits. For imperial power to grow, for example by expanding the markets for colonial products such as sugar and tobacco, traders from rival empires demanded spaces where the normal rule of law was partially suspended.

The establishment of free ports on colonized islands was the imperial answer to this demand. Some laws still applied, such as the protection of private property and contract enforcement. But otherwise, restrictions on who could trade what with whom were largely removed, as were most taxes. From these island settings, the term "offshore" was born.

The entwined histories of colonialism and offshore finance originate here, with selective freedom from the rule of law. But the connection did not end with free ports. Over the centuries, the two systems remained tightly linked, perhaps most visibly in the era of decolonization in the 1960s and 1970s. The contemporary system of offshore finance retained and built on the legal, financial, and social structures left behind by the retreating colonial powers. This has made the offshore system an engine for reproducing many of the ills of colonialism in modern form, supercharging illicit resource extraction along with the ever-widening inequalities of wealth, gender, and race.

The cost to society is enormous. Economists like Zucman estimate that flows of private individuals' wealth to offshore companies, trusts, and foundations cost nations of the world *at least* $110 billion each year in lost tax revenue, plus untold amounts of stolen foreign aid and other proceeds of corruption. Another $500 billion is lost each year due to multinational firms' use of offshore. Depriving states of the tax revenues needed to provide essential public services—such as public transportation, health-care infrastructure, and housing—degrades quality of life and opportunities for everyone. That lost $700 billion could have paid for a lot of hospitals, road improvements, public housing, and child-care centers. Such infrastructure is essential to economic development, promoting upward mobility and social stability.

But that's not all. In addition to depriving societies of the essential services and economic development that lead to upward mobility, the use of offshore by the ultra-rich and corporations imposes an unacknowledged burden on the rest of us. More than twenty years ago, Charles Rossotti, who was then the commissioner of the U.S. Internal Revenue Service, estimated that average taxpayers are subjected to a 15 percent surcharge to make up for what the ultra-rich aren't paying. It is a consummate irony that a country whose creation story centers on the revolt of citizens against tax injustice—the Boston Tea Party—now tolerates paying an involuntary and undisclosed subsidy to support tax avoidance by the wealthiest members of society.

The surcharge Rossotti estimated is almost certainly higher now, since—despite receiving dramatic tax cuts in 2017—the wealthiest Americans are making more aggressive use of offshore than ever. Recently, Zucman and his colleague Emmanuel Saez documented a dramatic increase in illegal activity by high earners in the United States: even as their tax rates decreased, they nearly *doubled* their rates of tax evasion. By 2018, the top 1 percent of earners were evading 20 to 25 percent of the income tax they owed.

Other new research using IRS audit data shows that a full 21 percent of the income of the most affluent Americans goes unreported and untaxed, and that a significant portion of that is due to "the concealment of offshore wealth." Of all the unpaid federal income tax in the United States, 36 percent is directly attributable to the top 1 percent of earners. If they were simply to pay the taxes they owe—not more tax, only what is due under present-day law—that would generate $175 *billion* in additional funds each year. By some estimates, that's enough to lift every American out of poverty.

This illustrates why offshore finance isn't just relevant to rich people: the uses of offshore finance affect what is and is not possible in our societies. From the way offshore finance leaves us overtaxed and underserved by government, you'd think We the People would be up in arms. But most don't see the connection between offshore and the declining quality and quantity of public services they receive. The offshore financial system and the people who use it have been very successful at shrouding their activities in secrecy.

Even in this era of widespread surveillance, the transfer of private wealth to offshore companies, trusts, and foundations has remained obscure. Far more is known about the global pathways of illegal arms and drug trafficking than about asset flows from onshore to offshore. Not only that, but it's exceptionally difficult to study the aspect of economic inequality most germane to offshore finance and most consequential for society, which is wealth, as opposed to income. While social movements like Occupy Wall Street galvanized public awareness of "the 1 percent" of top income earners, most of the problems associated with economic inequality actually stem from *wealth*: meaning the sum total of a person's assets (including the value of savings, investments, property, and business ownership) minus any debts.

It's that figure, also known as "net worth," that creates the long-term problems. Income inequalities don't necessarily lead to negative outcomes at the societal level, because they're often temporary, like an annual bonus or a lottery windfall. But wealth is far more stable than income. Wealth can be inherited, locking in capital and unearned advantages over generations. Such enduring structural advantages interfere with free markets and democracy, as well as meritocratic access to education, jobs, and political power.

That's why the Founding Fathers were so keen to abolish many forms of inherited wealth. Thomas Jefferson banned not only titles of nobility in the new United States but also the forms of dynastic wealth concentration that underpinned the nobility in the first place: specifically, entail and primogeniture, the centuries-old practices ensuring that land and other assets would be passed down indivisibly to the eldest male in a family. This was driven by Jefferson's conviction, as he put it in his *Autobiography*, that America needed "instead of an aristocracy of wealth, of more harm and danger, than benefit, to society, to make an opening for the aristocracy of virtue and talent." Thomas Paine, a political philosopher whose ideas influenced the Declaration of Independence and the U.S. Constitution, was a friend of Jefferson's and shared his view that entrenched wealth was antithetical to democracy. Thus, Paine advocated for a progressive annual wealth tax with a top rate of 100 percent. About 140 years later, as Congress debated the creation of permanent federal income and inheritance taxes, legislators were still raising the alarm, warning that "the Nation must protect itself from the menace of abnormal fortunes" bequeathed across generations.

These claims about wealth's threats to democracy have been borne out, not just in America but worldwide, by the confluence in recent years of declining democracy and rising wealth inequality. One of the experts I interviewed—a Cambridge-educated historian turned Cayman Islands wealth manager—took a positively grim view of the snowball effect of tax avoidance and inheritance that he'd observed over his international career. "Extremely wealthy people," he said, "are able to structure their affairs in such a way that they are able to pay much less tax than they would if my work and my industry didn't exist. And once you get a head start growing wealth, that lead is going to keep growing, progressive taxation and redistributive policy notwithstanding." To my surprise, he added rather ominously that "it becomes increasingly difficult with time to reverse these inequalities, short of revolution." But people can't revolt against a problem they don't know exists. That's where the secrecy, invisibility, and complexity that have shrouded offshore finance for decades have proved indispensable in protecting the system.

Indeed, the true extent and consequences of present-day wealth inequality are among the most important secrets that the offshore financial system is designed to conceal. While governments track income as part of their taxation systems, and some parts of those data are public, in many parts of the world wealth can be made administratively invisible—unrecorded, unaffiliated to the real owner, and, as a result, nearly untaxed and unregulated. Providing this cloak of invisibility is a key function of the offshore system. This is particularly true of private individual wealth, less so of corporate wealth. Firms are subject to far more regulation and disclosure requirements than individuals, even offshore.

The true extent of wealth inequality is "politically dangerous" information, as French sociologist Monique Pinçon-Charlot observed twenty-five years ago: a secular "taboo" enforced by data access limitations. Even trusted sources, like the popular Survey of Consumer Finances, which oversamples well-to-do households, are limited in the insight they can provide "because at high wealth levels the usual sources of wealth data—the official household surveys—become increasingly unreliable." Furthermore, as I learned from interviewing wealth managers, some individuals pay professional fixers to keep their names off the Forbes 400 and other "rich lists." While widely cited, the Forbes 400 list offers a highly inaccurate picture of the ultra-wealthy, since it counts only wealth from recorded sources, such as stocks in publicly traded corporations. This excludes assets like trust funds and ownership of firms that don't sell shares to the public, which are the majority of companies worldwide.

This scarcity of information may be a factor in the recent finding by economic psychologists that most people have no concept of the true levels of economic inequality in their countries. For example, Americans underestimate the real extent of wealth inequality by 42 percent. Physical segregation of rich and poor in their places of work and residence facilitates this lack of awareness. It's difficult to grasp how the other half lives if your paths never cross. But it is also a consequence of a deliberate strategy on the part of the ultra-rich, using offshore's heightened secrecy services to conceal the real extent of the chasm that has opened up between elites and the rest of us.

The notion of politically dangerous information is not new; but the offshore system is always inventing new ways to hide it. These innovations have created novel threats to both democracy and capitalism, which depend on accurate information circulating freely among voters and investors. Max Weber, a founding father of modern social science, noted this problem a century ago: the bureaucrats of his native Prussia only published statistics that made them look good, burying the rest to avoid political opposition.

Today, as back then, secrecy works not just through concealment but through fragmentation and the use of jargon that might as well be a secret code. In ancient Persia, Weber wrote, the shah's accountants kept their ledgers in a code known only to themselves, making the full extent of the ruler's wealth a state secret. Simmel observed similar strategies in use among criminal gangs as well as secret societies for aristocrats; modern research on terrorist networks and the Mafia echoes his findings. As Princeton University sociologist Matthew Desmond has observed, "Complexity is the refuge of the powerful." The offshore financial system has simply added contemporary legal-financial sophistication to this age-old strategy.

What about all the offshore leaks of the past few years? Whistleblowers who expose politically dangerous information shift the balance of power away from the secret keepers and toward the public interest. A few become household names, like Daniel Ellsberg, a military analyst who revealed the U.S. role in extending the Vietnam War by releasing the Pentagon Papers. Other whistleblowers have exposed the harms done by fossil fuels and tobacco. In the case of offshore finance, whistleblowers who went to the press using their real names, such as Hervé Falciani of Swiss Leaks and Antoine Deltour of LuxLeaks, have been punished severely: hounded for years through the courts and sentenced to prison. Their successors, like the "John Doe" who released the Panama Papers, have understandably chosen to remain anonymous. Together, all these leakers have made an unprecedented volume of confidential offshore client data available to the public. But while the information has in many cases been explosive—revealing that even trusted figures, such as the late Queen Elizabeth II of England, concealed their wealth in offshore accounts—it remains highly fragmented and incomplete. Until more information becomes available to provide context, there is no way to know how accurately any of the leaked data reflect the scope and significance of the secrets being kept offshore.

For example, the data constituting the 2016 Panama Papers leak (11.5 million documents, representing 2.6 terabytes of data) originated from one organization: the Panamanian law firm Mossack Fonseca. The 2017 Paradise Papers leak (13.4 million documents, representing 1.4 terabytes of data) came from just two organizations: the Bermuda law firm Appleby and the Hong Kong corporate service firm Asiaciti Trust. The Pandora Papers leak of 2021 (11.9 million documents, representing 2.9 terabytes of data) somewhat improved upon this problem by sourcing data from fourteen different organizations providing offshore financial services. The organizations, based in eight different countries, include law firms, corporate service providers, trust companies, and consultancies. While this latest leak sheds more light than ever before on this secretive realm, it still represents only a minuscule proportion of the thousands of offshore service providers and dozens of offshore financial centers in operation.

If offshore finance is really a threat to society, you might wonder why the authorities don't simply shut it down—as hundreds of economists, journalists, and policymakers have recommended. But the offshore system has proven remarkably robust, resisting every attempt to constrain it and the damage it inflicts on economies, democracies, and the natural environment. Shutting it down entirely would mean ending the secrecy that surrounds the offshore holdings of the wealthy and powerful, many of whom—as the Panama, Paradise, and Pandora Papers showed—are themselves heads of state, or finance ministers, or otherwise in a position of decision-making authority over legal and financial systems. Their conflicts of interest militate against using their power to curtail or end a system that benefits them so richly.

For example, while David Cameron was prime minister of the United Kingdom, he famously railed against British celebrities who used offshore accounts to dodge taxes. But when the Panama Papers broke, the world learned that Cameron himself had concealed from British voters that he was the beneficiary of an offshore trust based in Panama City. Five years later, the Pandora Papers revealed that Czech prime minister Andrej Babiš—who had come to power as an anti-corruption campaigner—was laundering tens of millions of dollars he'd acquired through tax fraud, using a string of secret offshore structures in the British Virgin Islands, the United States, and Monaco to buy seaside villas in the south of France. Many similar cases have come to light since the big offshore leaks began in 2016, and future leaks will undoubtedly reveal many more.

In addition to these conflicts of interest among individual politicians, there is also a fundamental reluctance among some nations to relinquish their share of the lucrative offshore financial services business. For many countries, particularly postcolonial states with small geographic territories or narrow economic bases—meaning few natural or human resources from which to generate an economy—being part of the offshore financial system represents an important source of income. They earn considerable fees not only from transactions and administration, such as corporate registrations, but also from the payroll taxes generated by local jobs created in the financial services industry. The British Virgin Islands (BVI), for example, reports on its official government website that more than half the country's gross domestic product (GDP) comes from providing offshore financial services; locals estimate that the figure is more like 70 percent of the national economy. Another former British colony, the Indian Ocean island of Mauritius, started providing offshore financial services about twenty years after the BVI, but selling secrecy now constitutes about 14 percent of its national economy—more than agriculture, forestry, or fishing.

But this isn't just a phenomenon of small or developing countries. It also happens in the wealthiest countries in the world. Many national and state governments have come to regard the provision of offshore financial services as essential parts of their economies. Because most of the world's offshore financial flows pass through London and New York, both the United Kingdom and United States have fought hard to keep as much foreign capital in their jurisdictions as possible. For example, both countries use tax and profit incentives to make it extremely attractive for foreigners to buy real estate there, and to establish corporations and trusts to hold their assets. Lawmakers argue that this benefits citizens in indirect ways: while the foreigners don't pay much (or anything) in taxes, they do pay fees, employ locals, and drive up property values, enriching locals who already own real estate.

For this reason, the business model of offshore finance has proven attractive to U.S. states with fragile economic bases, like Delaware and South Dakota. Much like postcolonial island nations, these states have little independent means to generate revenue, so they have loosened their regulations to make their jurisdictions appealing to foreign capital. While Delaware is most famous as a corporate tax haven, it also competes to attract the business of high-net-worth individuals, as does South Dakota. When these and a handful of other states changed their regulations to remove the time limit on trust funds (a highly secretive method of shielding wealth from taxes, debts, and other claims), they pulled in an additional $6 billion each in assets, generating an average 20 percent increase in business revenues for financial services professionals.

Meanwhile, New York and Florida have been so successful in attracting real estate purchases from foreigners in search of offshore tax breaks and legal protections that the U.S. Department of Treasury had to issue an alert in early 2023: Russian oligarchs were hiding their assets from American sanctions in those states' luxury property markets. That is, U.S. states were helping foreign nationals circumvent both federal law and American foreign policy. As this example illustrates, offshore financial services are so lucrative for some that they have created a chaotic policy landscape. While presidents and federal agencies issue sanctions and attempt to crack down on offshore finance, the U.S. financial services industry refuses to cooperate. Patriotism and national cohesion are no match for the vast sums to be made undermining the international rule of law.

This is a microcosm of a global problem. Shutting down or restricting offshore finance would require international coordination and cooperation. But such unity has been elusive for decades because the status quo is so profitable for a few. Plus, there is no central control mechanism to enforce cross-national cooperation. Even broadly multinational organizations that have tried to rein in offshore abuses—like the thirty-eight-member Organization for Economic Cooperation and Development (OECD) or the European Parliament, with twenty-seven member states—have had only limited success.

In sociology, we have a term for this kind of challenge: a collective action problem. It happens when individual entities—be they people, organizations, or nations—think they'll gain more from going it alone than from cooperation. The United States exemplified this thinking in 2014 when the Obama administration declined to cooperate with a new OECD policy initiative to crack down on offshore tax evasion. The policy, called the Common Reporting Standard (CRS), sounded innocuous enough: it required participating nations to join in the automatic exchange of information with each other concerning individual wealth held in the countries' financial institutions. The goal was to make it easier to spot tax cheats and money launderers as they moved money around the world—similar to the way U.S. law enforcement agencies share databases across state lines, the better to catch criminals on the run.

But when it came to fighting international financial crime, the Obama administration wouldn't join more than one hundred other countries in signing on to the OECD initiative. Publicly, the reason given was redundancy and cost: a report from the U.S. Government Accountability Office stated that the IRS already had all the tools it needed to stop tax cheats, and that joining the CRS might "generate additional costs and reporting burdens to U.S. financial institutions." Those extra administrative costs might have seemed like a small price to pay given what could be recouped from better enforcement: a 2023 paper by economists from Harvard and the Department of the Treasury shows that every dollar the IRS spends auditing the wealthy yields $12 in new tax revenue. But numerous independent analyses have suggested that the *costs* of compliance with the CRS were never the real issue. Instead, they posit, the problem was all the *profits* the U.S. financial services industry might lose, because joining the OECD initiative would make their offshore services less secretive and hence less appealing to foreigners. In the words of one Zurich-based wealth manager, refusing to cooperate allowed the United States to remain "awash" with foreign wealth so it could maintain a competitive advantage over other offshore centers.

Since its decision not to cooperate with other OECD countries in combatting offshore abuses, the United States has rocketed to the very top of the annual Financial Secrecy Index, which ranks nations according to which are "most complicit in helping individuals hide their finances from the rule of law." In 2013, the United States didn't even make the top five list of financial secrecy havens. But as of 2022, it was ranked number one worldwide, far outstripping Switzerland, Luxembourg, Hong Kong, and Singapore. For many of the global ultra-rich, the United States is now the premier destination for offshore finance.

CHAPTER 2

A Platform for Elite Insurgency

O NE OF THE MOST FASCINATING people I met while carrying out my offshore research was a bounty hunter. An Oxford-educated attorney by training, he helped create a thriving global industry in chasing down rich people who don't pay their debts. He and his London-based team spent hours scouring the social media of ultra-wealthy debt dodgers, so that they could be served with subpoenas and warrants for court proceedings—which the elites often evaded by disappearing on their private jets and yachts. I called him Boba Fett for the Jet Set.

The individuals he tracked down had purchased invisibility for themselves at great cost through the offshore financial system: that's where most of their fortunes were legally registered. But despite having secured private exit routes from many types of legal accountability, many of them kept sabotaging their own incognito in their quest for social status. In short, they liked to brag. On Instagram and Telegram, they posted photos of their hijinks at villas on the Mediterranean island of Sardinia, on the slopes at the French ski resort of Courchevel, and at other hot spots on the elite party circuit.

The bounty hunter tracked this public information, always ready to strike when the photos showed that deadbeat oligarchs had entered the United Kingdom. Then he or his colleagues could serve the required formal notice of the lawsuits against the defaulters, allowing the court proceedings to move forward. It was a satisfying job, he said, holding accountable people who were so accustomed to impunity that they practically taunted their creditors to catch them.

This tracked with what wealth managers had told me about their clientele. One practitioner I interviewed in the Cook Islands told me of a client who managed to pocket a half-million-dollar loan from Bank of America without ever repaying it by putting the money—plus most of his other assets—into a Cook Islands asset-protection trust and declaring bankruptcy. Because the client was not the legal owner of the assets in trust, Bank of America could not claw back any of the man's wealth in payment for that $500,000 loan. So, according to the wealth manager, the bank just walked away. Knowing that the Cook Islands "firewall" laws gave its attorneys almost no chance of prevailing in court, Bank of America wrote off the debt; the money stayed in the trust account, where the trustee (the legal owner of the assets) could dole it out as needed to pay the client's bills and keep him in style. The wealth manager expressed no moral view of this, only admiration for the client's masterful exploitation of the possibilities available under Cook Islands law. That's probably not the way most people would interpret this incident, but the ultra-rich and those who serve them aren't like most people. Many see themselves as deserving exemption from the rules that bind the rest of us as members of society.

Another practitioner I interviewed in Switzerland said that one of his clients belonged to a club of rich men who believe "that they are descended from the pharaohs and destined to inherit the earth." No surprise that such individuals would regard debt repayment as beneath their consideration. They were a *noblesse* without the *oblige*.

But while the ultra-rich expect to enjoy all the benefits of society without paying their fair share of the costs—or any costs, really—they don't want to do away with the rule of law altogether. They're all for laws protecting *their* property rights and enforcing *their* contracts, and of course they expect public goods like potable water, well-maintained roads, and police protection. They're just not keen on being *subject* to the law, doing their part to keep government up and running, or acknowledging their dependence on a free, functional society for their prosperity.

Recently, Howard Schultz—the billionaire former CEO of Starbucks—gave congressional testimony that perfectly encapsulated this complete disregard for the taxpayer-funded collective goods that made his individual success possible. Schultz testified that he "came from nothing," then acknowledged in the next breath that "I grew up in federally subsidized housing." Yes, he earned billions of dollars, but "No one gave it to me." Completely erased from his account is any acknowledgment of who paid for that subsidized housing or the roads, telecommunications infrastructure, banking system, and countless other public goods and institutions that allowed him to build wealth in the first place. Other Americans made those things and paid for them through their taxes. But you'd never know it from his "self-made man" story. Ironically, Schultz's fortune was linked to Starbucks's success at offshore tax avoidance: for over a decade, the firm used tax shelters in the Netherlands to avoid most U.K. and U.S. corporate tax, boosting the profits and share values to which Schultz's compensation was tied.

Of course, Schultz is by no means unique in this regard. He's just one of a whole cohort of contemporary billionaires beset by what even the pro-business stalwart *Financial Times* described—with evident exasperation—as "convenient amnesia" about the public investment that made their private wealth possible. Other examples include the vast fortunes of Google founders Sergey Brin and Larry Page, whose search engine development idea was funded in its infancy by tax dollars allocated by the U.S. National Science Foundation, and built atop the taxpayer-financed internet—originally created as a communication system for the Department of Defense.

Similarly, securities industry analysts note that Elon Musk is a billionaire only because of the massive taxpayer-funded subsidies he has received. A CNN report estimates that between 2008 and 2019, Musk benefited from at least $6.7 billion in federal cash infusions and regulatory credits to support his businesses, which were frequently on the verge of bankruptcy. Without that public assistance, "Musk wouldn't be the richest person in the world," one securities analyst told CNN. "It was really U.S. taxpayers that helped get him through his roughest time." Yet true to form, Musk used aggressive wealth management techniques in order to pay little or no tax for years, while vehemently opposing any legislation that might require billionaires to pay their fair share. For many elites like him, freedom mostly means the liberty not to be taxed.

Their rejection of mutual obligation is fundamentally indefensible, and thus urgently concealed—in part through the use of offshore finance. Paying tax is an act of social solidarity that underwrites other forms of solidarity; it is also a mechanism of social inclusion. When the offshore financial system allows some people (and corporations) to avoid paying tax, that doesn't just mean roads and hospitals and schools won't get built. It means that the most wealthy and powerful people in the world are playing "dine and dash" with the rest of us, skipping out on their share of the bill after benefiting from collective efforts to build a prosperous society.

One of the most corrosive aspects of the offshore financial system is the way it provides cover for this egregious rip-off. Before the offshore system existed in its present form, there were of course ultra-wealthy individuals. To quell dangerous levels of resentment and backlash, they usually tried to justify themselves morally through good works and contributions to the public good. Thus, 550 years ago in Florence, the Medici laundered their reputations and staved off public outrage over accusations of usury—then a mortal sin in the Roman Catholic Church—by funding the great works of art that launched the Renaissance. Later, American steel and railroad barons like Andrew Carnegie and Leland Stanford founded great universities and funded hundreds of libraries open to the public.

As the Panama, Paradise, and Pandora Papers show, those days of *noblesse oblige* are largely over. It's not just that the ultra-rich can use offshore to shield their fortunes from many of the mutual obligations that the rest of us take for granted, like paying our taxes and debts. It's that the secrecy they purchase with those shell corporations, trusts, and foundations allows them to escape most of the public scrutiny and condemnation that might deter such decisions.

That is why the cloak of invisibility provided by offshore finance is so desirable to the world's wealthiest people. It conceals both the real extent of economic and political inequality and its source: a radical and deeply unpopular agenda that is not just anti-democratic and opposed to the rule of law but also surprisingly anti-capitalist. As social scientists and historians have noted, economic arrangements in the offshore world resemble feudalism in some key respects, creating dynastic con-centrations of wealth that undermine important features of capitalism, including entrepreneurship and the free flow of capital.

In fact, some historians point out that the offshore world isn't really new in its aims. Rather, it represents an effort to return to pre-Enlightenment forms of economic and political control: what Cornell historian Raymond Craib calls "a 'Restoration' of elite power akin to that of the return of the French monarchy in 1815." Designed to resist both comprehension and control by outsiders, the offshore financial system has become the global platform for this counterrevolution.

The present-day offshore world also bears an uncanny resemblance to the seventeenth-century heyday of piracy in the Atlantic Ocean, in which "plunder economies" arose from the aggressive theft perpetrated by figures like Henry Morgan, namesake of the well-known Captain Morgan rum brand. His method of wealth accumulation based on international networks of theft and predation survived only because there were places to cache the plunder: depots known as "pirate nests." On the peripheries of colonial outposts—including in American mainland and Caribbean colonies that later became offshore financial centers—local elites often helped the pirates protect their ill-gotten wealth from the law back in their home countries, in return for a share of the spoils.

It was a good living from the pirates' point of view, but would you call it capitalism? Most economists would not. The late Austrian economist Friedrich von Hayek—Nobel laureate and icon of libertar-ian thought—argued that capitalism could survive only in an envi-ronment where honesty, fairness, and respect for private property were enforced by social norms and law. In contrast, the value propo-sition of offshore finance depends on *un*fairness and *dis*honesty: the secrecy offshore provides enables deception about who really owns what, creating an escape route from the rule of law. This is fundamentally opposed to what economists since Adam Smith have defined as essential preconditions for capitalism. While dishonesty and unfairness can occur in free markets, classical economic theory regards them as disturbances that market equilibrium will ultimately punish and expel—for example, by putting fraudulent or predatory traders out of business.

Offshore finance survives and thrives based on a logic of predation rather than of capitalism. It might look like capitalism, because it is possible for some to pursue profits and maximize economic self-interest. But the system is optimized for gaming the laws of other countries and for hoarding capital, rather than for putting capital to productive use.

As Joseph Schumpeter—another famous Austrian economist—put it, capitalism necessitates "creative destruction." Among other things, that means there must inevitably be risks and losses for capitalists. While that's personally bad for those individuals who sustain the losses, it's vital to perpetuating the health and vitality of the economic system. As change occurs through competition and innovation, the failure of old business models frees up capital to circulate in the economy so that it can be used by entrepreneurs. This circulation prevents excessive concentration of wealth and power in a few hands, which both von Hayek and Schumpeter viewed as a kiss of death for capitalist dynamism. Offshore finance, however, makes it possible for the ultra-wealthy to escape many of these risks and losses, and to grow richer at an accelerated rate. This may be why billionaire PayPal founder Peter Thiel—who once penned an op-ed for the *Wall Street Journal* titled "Competition Is for Losers"—has been so keen to fund the creation of new offshore tax havens.

In essence, the ultra-rich use offshore as a kind of financial "safe space" for themselves, in which they are permitted to take reckless risks and pocket the profits when they pay off. But if things go wrong, the same system allows them to offset their losses onto others, in the form of taxpayer-funded bailouts. It's a "heads I win, tails you lose" world. Billionaires like Thiel use the protections of the offshore system to make a mockery of capitalist competition. As economists Anastasia Nesvetailova and Ronen Palan have noted, many contemporary fortunes arise not from creating value but rather from elites *sabotaging* regulators with one hand and looting the public purse with the other.

The 2008 global financial crisis exemplified this economic model. The collapse originated with the failure of two offshore hedge funds based in the Cayman Islands. Even by financial industry standards, the funds had taken on reckless amounts of debt and risk trading in barely regulated securities that few people understood. MIT finance professor Andrew Lo called them "among the most secretive of financial institutions," and this was key to their destructive potential. With minimal transparency or oversight, the Caymans incubated the seeds of a catastrophe whose impact reached far beyond the economic realm. While some early assessments sought to absolve offshore hedge funds of their role in the subprime mortgage crisis and shift the blame to banks, more recent work by economists from the U.S. Federal Reserve points to the crucial role the funds played, both as the initial trigger for the crisis and, later, in the systemic amplification of risk in the global economy.

The damage offshore hedge funds unleashed was nearly apocalyptic: "unique in terms of the wealth destruction," according to the International Monetary Fund. The 2008 financial crisis ultimately wiped out $50 trillion in value—equivalent to one full year of *global* GDP, meaning the total worth of all the goods and services produced by the entire world over a twelve-month period. Millions worldwide were driven to homelessness by layoffs and evictions; thousands took their lives. Average U.S. households needed a full decade to recover the wealth they lost during 2008 and 2009. But the financial services industry, which caused the crisis in the first place? The U.S. part of that industry secured a taxpayer-funded bailout of $700 billion with no strings attached. The money was intended by Congress to help banks stop foreclosing on homes and restart lending, thereby halting the economy's free fall. Instead, many financial institutions used the funds to pay bonuses to personnel, including the traders who had triggered the crisis.

Mirroring the scarcity of prosecutions and convictions following the Panama Papers and subsequent offshore leaks, there was virtually no accountability for the crisis. Just one top banker involved in the sub-prime mortgage meltdown went to jail; the others walked away scot-free and, in many cases, a great deal richer than before. Only about half the firms that received a bailout repaid the federal government. Meanwhile, the Federal Reserve estimates that the crisis wiped out about $70,000 in lifetime income for every American.

Not for the first time, some of the most powerful people in society displaced onto the rest of us the costs incurred by their reckless risks. The result is what the late American political scientist Michael Harrington (no relation) called "socialism for the rich." What many observers of this phenomenon have failed to note is how often this profound inequity now originates offshore, where lack of regulation and taxation makes it easy to generate risks and reap outsized profits. Secrecy then enables the perpetrators to avoid legal and financial accountability. This, in turn, interferes with the market signaling and discipline necessary for capitalism to function.

So while some scholars have characterized offshore finance as a realm of "ultra-capitalism," the evidence suggests the opposite conclusion. Wealthy individuals (and firms) use the offshore system precisely to *avoid* capitalism's risks and market corrections. Most capitalists don't need to conceal their identities in business dealings. But offshore, it's standard procedure for firms to hire nominee shareholders and nominee directors: people who rent their names for use in corporate registers, so that the true identities of a corporation's owners and decision-makers remain secret. This is in no way necessary to conduct legitimate business activity, but it's very useful for escaping losses and liabilities to investors, creditors, customers, and regulators. That's not capitalism: it's just cheating.

Cheating, in turn, tends to create concentrations of wealth that become dynastic—enough to enable future generations to exempt themselves from market forces through inheritance. These monopolies of wealth, whether familial or corporate, are incompatible with the dynamism and capital mobility required for capitalism to thrive. As Mills wrote in *The Power Elite*, "Wealth not only tends to perpetuate itself, but . . . tends also to monopolize opportunities for getting 'great wealth.'" At the same time, it renders the rest of us poorer by reducing the tax base that supports education, transportation, and health and housing services. As a result, fewer people are equipped to innovate and fewer still can afford to take the risks necessary to start new ventures; entrepreneurship declines into stagnation. A century from now, as economists like Thomas Piketty have shown, the richest members of society will simply be the descendants of today's wealthiest people—a return to quasi-feudal conditions.

The reduction of capital flow and the stagnation in upward mobility caused by keeping wealth in the hands of the same families over generations have long been identified as antithetical to capitalism. These problems were central to Max Weber's theory about why capitalism arose when and where it did: among a fringe group of Calvinist merchants in Western Europe, rather than in the seemingly more promising environment of the great trading empires of Asia, Africa, and the Middle East. The Ottoman Empire, for example, would seem fertile ground for capitalism to have emerged, thanks to the fabulous wealth it accumulated from commercial networks that spanned three continents and brought the coffee and tulip bulb crazes to Europe in the seventeenth century.

What held the Ottomans back, Weber wrote, was not any lack of commercial acumen but their invention of the *vakf*: a legal structure that allowed wealth to be locked up in the hands of elite families, generation after generation. While the *vakf* was supposed to consolidate capital for charitable purposes, its use as a means of transmitting wealth through inheritance helped to create a rentier class among the Ottoman elite. This meant that they lived on income from property and investments, without creating any new value in the economy. The result was stagnation instead of the dynamism required by capitalism. "The very persistent immobilization of accumulated wealth in the form of *vakfs*," Weber wrote, "was of very great importance for the economic development of the Orient . . . which used accumulated wealth as a source of rent, not as acquisitive capital."

Later scholarship has been more explicit, pinning centuries of underdevelopment in the Middle East specifically on the institution of the *vakf*. That's because the *vakf* didn't just concentrate wealth: it placed private fortunes *outside state control*, just as offshore financial structures do now. As a result, everyone was worse off, though a few seemed to enjoy fabulous wealth. In the words of the contemporary Turkish American economist Timur Kuran, the *vakf* "locked vast resources" away from the market and from state-led development that might have transformed the region into a capitalist powerhouse. The *vakf* is also thought to have inspired the invention of the common-law trust in England during the Middle Ages: a structure later blamed for tying up too much wealth among the landed gentry, delaying capitalist development in that country for centuries. In fact, the contemporary surge in the use of trusts as part of the global expansion of offshore finance has amplified many of the economic and social problems associated with these structures.

As harmful as offshore finance is to capitalism, its threat to democracy is arguably even greater. The two phenomena are related: the economic power that can be amassed through the offshore system gives a small group of individuals outsized leverage vis-à-vis state power. For example, a former economic adviser to the government of the Channel Island of Jersey—one of the world's most popular tax havens—reported that "superwealthy people . . . can actually negotiate the tax rates they pay" by arranging secret deals with island officials. Although Jersey's top tax bracket is set at only 20 percent, private agreements allow some to pay just a fraction of that, or to pay no tax at all. This creates conditions in which some nations offer representation without taxation and made-to-order laws for a small group of ultra-rich individuals who don't even live there.

These wealthy individuals' backroom deals may seem like relatively harmless self-interest, until you consider the power they have to realize their ambitions. Many of the wealth managers I interviewed warned of client ideologies and offshore strategies that were openly antithetical to democracy. One Zurich-based practitioner specializing in clients worth $50 million or more told me her clients were

> people above nationality and laws: maybe they're only .2% of the world population, but they have enormous power. . . . Money is nothing to them; they seek to influence the world around them, and they bend politics and politicians to their wishes. It's potentially very dangerous.

In this way, offshore finance has been corroding democracy for decades. The damage wasn't widely recognized until recently because the countries it harmed first were usually smaller and still operating in the shadow of imperial power. This includes places like the Channel Island of Jersey, where a nominally parliamentary system dating back to the thirteenth century was co-opted by the financial services industry and its ultra-rich clients, most of whom will never set foot on the island. In the 1950s, attorneys on Jersey spotted an opportunity to profit from the United Kingdom's 80 percent inheritance tax and rising taxes on income: Brits who moved their assets to financial institutions in Jersey (a distance of just eighty-five miles from England) could avoid all those taxes. The experts in Jersey hoped that this gambit would trigger a revival of the island's economy, thanks to the influx of cash from fees paid by wealthy foreigners and the creation of new jobs to serve them. It seemed like a win-win for Jersey, and for a while it really was, with the island enjoying almost full employment and a per capita national income higher than that of the United Kingdom or the United States.

But as Jersey natives like John Christensen have documented, the island's politicians soon became arms of its finance industry, ensuring that laws were passed and enforced mainly to suit the interests of the international clients—sometimes against the interests and wishes of the local population. The island became a favorite hiding place for the ill-gotten wealth of South Africans enriched by the apartheid regime, as well as the looted wealth of newly privatized Russian industries in the hands of oligarchs and the hundreds of millions of dollars' worth of bribes and kickbacks collected by Nigerian dictator Sani Abacha.

By the time the global financial crisis hit in 2008, the endless tax breaks for foreigners had left a crater so big in Jersey's national economy that public services like schools and roads were in steep decline. There was also political unrest, driven by Jersey's middle class being forced to assume what the country's former finance minister admitted was an "excessive burden" of taxation. This is by no means an unusual trajectory for the fiscal paradises of the world: in fact, it's the norm, repeated across the Caribbean, the South Pacific, and wherever sufficiently wealthy individuals can afford to purchase secrecy and bespoke laws from struggling postcolonial democracies. Thus, British Ghanaian legal scholar Kojo Koram summarized the political economy of offshore as "a semi-feudal arrangement which corporate interests have used to dampen expressions of mass democracy."

Some ultra-wealthy clients of the offshore financial system amass so much political influence that, like warlords, they gain the power to destabilize countries—particularly in the smaller offshore centers whose economies are most dependent on foreign capital. Increasingly, that power is making itself felt in developed countries as well, fomenting violent protests in Europe and the United States, and producing headlines such as "Tax Cheats Fuel Right-Wing Extremism Around the World" in mainstream publications like the *Week*.

The Panama Papers leak of April 2016 and the Paradise Papers of November 2017 showed that several of the most prominent supporters of Brexit held substantial assets offshore, in accounts that included contributions from both Russian and American oligarchs. These later came under investigation as conduits for illegal foreign influence on the British referendum. For example, U.S. hedge fund manager Robert Mercer created a $60 million "war chest" to fund both the Brexit campaign and Donald Trump's 2016 presidential campaign—political projects that, ironically, were cast as efforts to "restore popular control" over government against "globalists" and "foreign elites."

The leaks also exposed France's Jean-Marie Le Pen, founder of the political dynasty behind the anti–European Union party National Rally (formerly Front National), for having stashed millions in offshore accounts. His daughter Marine, who took over leadership of the party, later mounted a presidential campaign that included the promise of a Brexit-like referendum on withdrawing France from the European Union. The campaign was found to have been financed in part by Russian oligarchs, who funneled millions of euros through offshore accounts in Cyprus. Meanwhile the Financial Action Task Force—an international anti-corruption watchdog—found that Germany's far-right party was also funded through offshore accounts. The same pattern has been reported in the far-right politics of numerous other European countries.

In a national security memorandum issued a few months after his inauguration, President Biden declared that strengthening democracy around the world would be a priority of his administration, and that the United States would "lead by example and . . . fight the scourge of corruption." Four months later, the Pandora Papers made clear that the United States had itself been a key facilitator of international financial corruption, to the detriment of democracy here and abroad. To attract the wealth of non-U.S. citizens, South Dakota, Nevada, Wyoming, and even Washington, D.C., have legislated special tax and secrecy rules for capital originating overseas. These rules have destabilized political economies globally and exposed a significant weakness in our own political institutions: vulnerability to influence by transnational outlaw capital.

The waning power of conventional state authority against off-shore finance was vividly illustrated when the United States and other countries sanctioned Russian oligarchs for their roles in facilitating the February 2022 invasion of Ukraine. In a striking display of impunity, several oligarchs eluded U.S. sanctions by using offshore vehicles to invest in U.S. real estate—right under the noses of the Biden administration. This included industrialist Oleg Deripaska, a confidant of Russian President Vladimir Putin's. Deripaska was already a serial offender, having found multiple ways to evade the sanctions that had followed his interference in the 2016 U.S. presidential election, when he'd illegally funneled $60 million to Donald Trump's campaign manager through accounts in Cyprus and the Cayman Islands.

Russian oligarchs have long used the offshore financial system to commit financial crimes, both domestic and international. And they have led the international community on a merry chase, with the United States, European Union, and United Kingdom always seeming one step behind: seize or freeze Russian assets here, and the wealth ends up over there, in a different offshore center. This only enhances the international reputation the oligarchs have cultivated as untouchable elites.

Of course, Russians aren't the only ones doing this: smaller versions of their kleptocratic political economy have been built and used by the ultra-rich from Asia, Africa, Latin America, and Eastern Europe. The global pattern is that the more autocratic the country, the more of its national wealth—expressed as a proportion of GDP—is held offshore. The UAE, Saudi Arabia, Venezuela, and Russia top the rankings in this regard, holding offshore wealth equivalent to more than 50 percent of their countries' total economies, compared to the global average of 10 percent. Among the very richest households in those countries, the top .01 percent, Russian elites lead the world in their use of offshore, holding around 60 percent of their private wealth there. Because of this scale of offshore activity, and the uses to which it has been put, the Russian kleptocratic machine is the best developed in the world and the one best understood by investigators.

In one particularly egregious case, Russian oligarchs ran between $20 and $80 billion in looted public funds through a "laundromat" of offshore accounts, many in the United States and the United Kingdom. While a Moldovan businessman and a Russian banker were tried and imprisoned for these crimes, the elites who benefited were never punished. When oligarchs are caught in money-laundering and sanctions-evasion schemes, they typically avoid punishment by using offshore accounts to transfer their assets to their children, spouses, siblings, or most-trusted friends. Putin himself exemplifies this strategy: the Panama Papers showed that his childhood friend—classical cellist Sergei Roldugin—owns what a U.S. Congress report characterizes as "offshore companies valued at $2 billion that are suspected fronts for stashing pilfered wealth" belonging to Putin himself.

This kind of elite lawlessness, which escapes the authority of any national or multinational governance, represents just as much of a threat to the international order as other forms of militancy and radicalism. While most studies of "extremist violence" concern criminal gangs or terrorist organizations, secretive networks of offshore finance are linked to a different kind of extremism—perhaps best captured in the phrase "libertarian anarchism." Adherents to that ideology consider it an offense to liberty that they are obliged to repay their debts, pay their fair share of the costs of society through taxes, or otherwise obey the laws of the land. Offshore is a refuge from what these elites see as society's illegitimate claims on them and their wealth.

Many of the wealth managers I interviewed were sympathetic to this view and happy to facilitate their clients' escape from the long arm of the law. One practitioner in Dubai spoke of protecting his clients from "rapacious governments." Another in the United States explained, "Many of our clients live in countries where theft of your assets without due process is common, and that includes confiscatory tax regimes. It's state-sponsored theft, and we are among the very few who will stand up to that." Their viewpoint was seemingly shared by the global professional society for wealth managers, the Society of Trust and Estate Practitioners (STEP). The course books for my credential training program were peppered with phrases like "Onerously high, *some may say unethical*, tax demands," and other language challenging the legitimacy of state demands on "wealth creators." At one professional society meeting in 2010, I watched an officer of STEP describe the U.K. tax authorities as the "robber barons of the Inland Revenue." The remark was greeted with nods and knowing chuckles from the hundreds of wealth managers in the audience.

Shared contempt for mutual obligation and the rule of law creates a distinct overlap between the well-heeled clientele of offshore finance, on the one hand, and criminals and terrorists on the other. In their uses of modern offshore finance, the two groups can be difficult to distinguish. As British journalist Nick Shaxson put it, "A peculiar mixture of characters populates this world: castle-owning members of ancient continental European aristocracies, fanatical supporters of American libertarian writer Ayn Rand, members of the world's intelligence services, global criminals, British public schoolboys, assorted lords and ladies and bankers galore. Its bugbears are government, laws, and taxes, and its slogan is freedom."

Adherents of this worldview believe that democracy is a failure, doomed—in the words of libertarian economist Hans-Hermann Hoppe—by "bums" and "pests" who aren't up to the challenge of self-government. There is a pronounced overlap between support for these ideas and for the use of offshore finance. For example, Peter Thiel and Robert Mercer are among Hoppe's most devoted adherents in the United States. They demand radical freedom for themselves, while backing authoritarians to rule over the rest of us.

This isn't just an American phenomenon. Worldwide, these elites— including dozens of current and former heads of state, as well as business leaders—are united by their contempt for and brazen defiance of democratic governance. The offshore financial system connects them in a shared project to escape constraints on their economic and political power. Moreover, the scores of presidents, monarchs, and ministers named in the Panama, Paradise, and Pandora Papers have abandoned the notion of national interest: by placing billions in unpaid taxes, stolen foreign aid, and the proceeds of crime into secret offshore structures, they enriched themselves at the expense of their countries. This includes not just anti-corruption campaigners, like Czechia's Andrej Babiš and Kenya's Uhuru Kenyatta, but trusted figureheads like the late Queen Elizabeth II of England. Though elites like these may not know one another personally, their uses of offshore position them in a shared space of opposition to legal, political, and economic equity. They create a political problem in democratic societies, where governance depends on legitimacy and the consent of the governed. Such political systems can't function when impunity becomes the ultimate status symbol. Elite lawlessness is a premodern privilege, incompatible with the principle of equality before the law.

Thus, government and corporate leaders who appear in the offshore leaks should be understood not just as corrupt people who got caught: they are elites in revolt, engaged in a political project of refusing obligation to the societies that allowed them to become wealthy and powerful. Elite exceptionalism has always been the animating principle of the offshore world, but until recently, *overt* proclamations of impunity were rare. The price of social and political prominence onshore included an obligation to simulate respect for ideals such as the common good and equality before the law. Offshore secrecy changed that, permitting an ethos of radical impunity to flourish and justify itself through its own surging wealth and power. Elites now openly refuse any obligation to the societies that allowed them to become wealthy and powerful: instead, they express radically anti-democratic and anti-egalitarian positions, without fear of sanction. For example, in a 2009 autobiographical essay titled "The Education of a Libertarian," Thiel wrote that American women getting the vote ruined democracy and capitalism alike:

> The 1920s were the last decade in American history during which one could be genuinely optimistic about politics. Since 1920, the vast increase in welfare beneficiaries and the extension of the franchise to women—two constituencies that are notoriously tough for libertarians—have rendered the notion of "capitalist democracy" into an oxymoron.

Thiel's fellow offshore enthusiast Robert Mercer allegedly holds similar views. While Mercer himself has almost never spoken to the press, his colleagues and co-workers of decades say he has bankrolled white supremacist political activities, views cats as more valuable than people, and "thinks society is upside down—that government helps the weak people get strong, and makes the strong people weak by taking their money away, through taxes."

Wealth managers I interviewed described similar views among their clients from all over the world. One elegant London-based practitioner who spoke with me described his clients almost as if they were being persecuted by the demands of modern democratic states. "Social democracy," said this white-haired gentleman with a signet ring and silk pocket square, "is creating too big demands on the wealth creators. . . . You can't get voted in now unless you support massive entitlement programs, because too many people receive them. With the result that governments now need an ever-increasing share of GDP from the producers to fulfill their promises. . . . This leads wealth creators to engage in the shadow economy, and so forth." In other words, he conceded that his wealthy clients were skirting the law or violating it outright—hence the euphemistic reference to "the shadow economy"—but couldn't be blamed for it. By his lights, democracy and taxation were the real villains.

The "wealth creators" he described were not just Americans but his entire clientele, composed primarily of Europeans and Latin Americans. The global convergence in views this wealth manager described points to what French sociologists Bruno Cousin and Sébastien Chauvin have described as an increasing "transnational homogenization of a wealth-based elite." The financial services industry reached that conclusion years earlier, with a 2005 research report segmenting the world into two types of people: "the Plutonomy and the rest."

This postnational perspective corresponds to the way most of the ultra-rich see themselves, according to the wealth managers I interviewed. As one Swiss practitioner said of the clients she and her colleagues served, "They all know each other" and they have "a lot more in common with each other than with the people of their own countries." They represented, she said, a transnational community with its own rules and culture, which are often hostile to the very concepts of democracy and competitive free markets. A German wealth manager—himself a member of the hereditary nobility—spoke of his clients as "this closed shop of wealthy people," using a term that comes from labor organizing to describe a workplace no one can join unless they are a union member. "Closed shop" signifies class solidarity and collective action. "The higher you go up on the economic pyramid," he added, "the smaller the group becomes, and the people went to business school together, they have known each other for decades, and they talk to each other."

What do they talk about? For one thing, they socialize and intermarry: an ancient strategy for concentrating dynastic wealth. One wealth manager in Singapore told me that he's become a literal matchmaker for his clients, arranging dates with people of similar fortunes and tastes. They also talk about their offshore financial strategies. One Swiss practitioner expressed frustration that his clients made decisions for their wealth based on what their friends were doing rather than on what was in their own financial interest: "They'll say, 'I want a Cayman or BVI company.' We explain why that's not a good idea, and they often say, 'I don't care: I want one; my friends have them.'" While the ultra-rich themselves rarely speak publicly on such matters, they occasionally describe a sort of invisible nation whose members recognize and coordinate with one another. As the billionaire American private equity investor Glenn Hutchins put it, "You see the same people, you eat in the same restaurants, you stay in the same hotels. But most important, we are engaged as global citizens in crosscutting commercial, political, and social matters of common concern." The offshore financial system links these ultra-wealthy globe-trotters structurally, through shared involvement in the international ecosystem of legal-financial secrecy.

Some elite clients of the offshore financial system literally see themselves as superhuman or semi-divine. This evocation of god-king status is by no means exceptional to the self-described descendants of the pharaohs mentioned at the beginning of this chapter. According to the wealth managers I interviewed, many high-net-worth individuals regard themselves as empowered to transcend time, space, and the laws of nature, too. This goes beyond the crackpots you might see in the news, like the U.S. tech billionaire who spends $2 million per year to "reverse aging," including infusing himself with the blood of his teenaged son. Less visibly but much more seriously, the wealthy are using the offshore financial system to extend their personalities and preferences beyond their lifetimes, as several practitioners told me. One said of his clients, "These are people who have everything they want— the only thing they don't have is immortality, and they really want it. They love the idea of a perpetual trust, and so what you usually end up doing with these clients is creating a perpetual trust with an intricately detailed letter of wishes, specifying that 'my grandson's second son gets X, but only if he does Y.' Very specific conditions, tight control."

These efforts to transcend time and gain omnipotence aren't limited to control over the families of the wealthy. The ambition of many of these elites is to reshape the world in their image. These ideas are enshrined in a popular libertarian text favored by users of the offshore system: *The Sovereign Individual*. The 1997 bestseller, which Thiel listed among his six favorite books, likens the ultra-rich to "the gods in Greek myth":

> Commanding vastly greater resources and beyond the reach of many forms of compulsion, the Sovereign Individual will redesign governments and reconfigure economies.

With its promise of impunity and world domination, this passage could serve as the mission statement for the offshore financial system.

CHAPTER 3

Zombie Colonialism

■　　　　■　　　　■　　　　■　　　　■　　　　■　　　　■

L ET ME TELL YOU THE story of a country transformed by con men, white-collar criminals, and latter-day pirates. They convened from former colonial outposts of the British Empire to transform a down-on-its-luck Caribbean trading post into a world-leading offshore financial center. They did it by repurposing the tools and tropes of colonialism to create a new empire of modern finance in the archipelago of seven hundred coral islands known as the Bahamas.

Such metamorphoses are the stuff of imperial immortality. Over centuries, regimes change and rearrange some of the building blocks of their predecessors, but the basic processes of expropriation and dispossession remain unchanged. You can see this for yourself up close in places where successive empires have visibly built upon their precursors' work, as in the Peruvian city of Cusco: the ancient Inca imperial capital of fabled wealth and religious significance. The city's temple to the sun god, Coricancha, was once a wonder of the world, with walls paneled in sheets of hammered gold and a garden filled with life-sized golden statues of alpacas. By the time I saw it at the age of twelve, all the gold was gone. Only a few of the giant walls remained—repurposed by the Spanish conquistadores, who had used the Incas' road system to conquer the city, then built their own temple (the church of Santo Domingo) directly atop Coricancha, using its original stones. I didn't know much about colonialism then, but that striking image of conquest made a lasting impression on me. I'd never realized that the tools of one empire could be used to construct a new one: not only in the same place but with the very same building blocks. Many years later, I realized that this was exactly how the offshore financial system had been built.

While the sun long ago set on the British Empire, its lineaments can still be clearly discerned in the offshore system today. Nearly every offshore financial center in the world—and there are dozens—is a former British colony. Economist Ronen Palan estimates that about 68 percent of offshore finance is based in current or former British territories; if we count the United States as a former colony, the figure rises to 83 percent. Why? Because the whole offshore system runs on the legal-financial infrastructure of the imperial era. It's an operating system repurposed for the benefit of a new elite: no longer the people of the British metropole, where the empire was headquartered, but a "stateless super-rich."

For scholars of colonialism, this is old news. As one put it, "While colonialism in its formal sense might have been dismantled, the colonial state has not." Though empires come and go, their legal-financial bureaucracies lurch along like the undead, extracting natural and human resources at the expense of locals. About one hundred and fifty years ago, Karl Marx famously remarked upon the vampire-like characteristics of capitalism. In the same spirit, offshore finance could be likened to zombie colonialism, since it operates through the decayed yet seemingly indestructible corpus of imperial infrastructure.

By the mid-twentieth century, it was evident that as an old empire was dying, a new one was being born. Martinican poet Aimé Césaire, a seminal theorist of colonialism and its impact, wrote in 1950 that "American high finance considers that the time has come to raid every colony in the world." It was an eerily prescient observation that coincided precisely with the opportunistic reconfigurations of power occurring in his native Caribbean. A rogues' gallery of modern-day buccaneers and pirates (many from the United States or financed by American dollars) rushed in to prey on the economic vulnerability and legal-financial resources of those increasingly self-governing states. Institutional entrepreneurs—mostly lawyers and financiers—emerged to scavenge the remains of colonial administration and create new configurations of power, much as the Spanish built their church in Cusco on and of the Inca temple.

But why did the British Empire loom so large in the creation of the offshore financial system, rather than the Spanish Empire or those of the other European imperial powers? The Spanish, after all, occupied a territory large enough to rival that of the British, from the Americas around the globe to the South Pacific; yet none of their former colonies became offshore centers. By the same token, none of the former French, Portuguese, German, or Italian colonies has any role in the contemporary offshore system, unless at some point, like the Indian Ocean islands of Mauritius and the Seychelles, they became British territories. Of the once globe-spanning and fabulously wealthy Dutch Empire, only two tiny islands—Aruba and Curaçao, off the northern coast of Venezuela—entered the offshore financial services industry, where they remain minor players. What accounts for this curious pattern?

Three factors were decisive in making the British Empire the birthplace of contemporary offshore finance: its tax system, its legal system, and its London-based administrators' distinctive strategy for pushing former colonies toward economic independence. By means of these rather abstract-sounding factors, the sophisticated modern network of fiscal paradises was built atop a foundation of raw, racialized colonial power. As legal scholar Kojo Koram put it recently in his analysis of the "afterlife" of British imperialism: "It is the protections that tax havens provide to transnational capital that are the real continuation of empire's dynamics of extraction and exploitation."

American readers raised on their country's founding story of a revolt against unjust and excessive taxation—the famous Boston Tea Party of 1773—may be surprised to learn how good the British colonists really had it. Unlike other imperial powers, the British kept taxes low in their colonies or eliminated taxes entirely, as an enticement for settlers to move there and stay. What tax burden existed was borne mostly by the native population. For example, the royal charter of 1629 that established the Massachusetts Bay Colony exempted settlers from all taxes related to trade with Britain for seven years, and from all other taxes for twenty-one years. Prior to the revolution of 1776, American colonists paid a tax rate of 1 to 1.5 percent, even as their compatriots back in Britain paid 5 to 7 percent. Shortly after the revolution, eager to avoid another colonial uprising, the British passed the Taxation of Colonies Act of 1778, which eliminated almost all taxes in the empire's North American territories, including the Caribbean islands.

This set the precedent for those colonies to become tax havens centuries later. As one historian described the fiscal policy of the British Empire: "Few organized governments taxed their people so lightly. . . . The colonists soon became accustomed to minimal taxation, and by the late colonial period they viewed low taxes as almost a birth-right." This expectation carried right up to the period of twentieth-century independence movements. In contrast, the Spanish taxed their colonies very heavily. Mexican colonists, for example, paid a full 50 percent *more* in taxes than their fellow imperial subjects back in Spain. Overall, the tax burden on Spanish colonists was thirty-five times higher than that faced by British colonists. This created historical path dependencies whose consequences are evident today in the imperial origins of offshore financial centers.

The empire's legal infrastructure was perhaps even more decisive in making the former British colonies a "privileged site of accumulation" in modern finance. The common-law tradition originated in England following the Norman Conquest of 1066 and eventually spread to all British territories, becoming the imperial "operating system" globally. Common law functions in a fundamentally different way from civil law: the tradition derived from the Romans, still dominant in continental European countries and their former colonies. Crucially, common law is less restrictive and much more flexible to innovation than civil law. This makes common law better suited to performing what legal schol-ars call the "tricks" for "manipulating facets of ownership" that make offshore secrecy possible. The civil-law system works like the children's game "Mother, May I," in that it spells out precisely what is permit-ted; everything else is by definition prohibited. Common law works in the opposite way: it establishes what is forbidden and implicitly per-mits everything else. Unlike in civil law, the boundaries between legal and illegal conduct can shift readily based on decisions of common-law judges in different times and jurisdictions. This allows offshore finan-cial centers to compete with one another by tailoring their laws to the changing needs of the ultra-wealthy.

It is technically possible to achieve some of these aims in a civil-law context—for example, through a Dutch *stichting*, a type of charitable foundation that billionaire IKEA founder Ingvar Kamprad used to protect his fortune from some forms of taxation. But the common-law tradition provides many more options, along with greater ease and privacy. A classic example is the common-law trust: an asset-holding structure that emerged in medieval England to help noblemen dodge taxes owed to the king. It is now a mainstay of personal and corporate finance worldwide, because it offers significant tax and secrecy advantages over alternative structures, like corporations and foundations.

Trusts are private agreements in which assets are legally owned by one person (the trustee) while being used by someone else (the beneficiary). In many countries, trusts are not required to register with the state, meaning they can exist in secret; in contrast, corporations and foundations must register and deliver periodic reports on their assets and governing personnel. Furthermore, unlike corporations and foundations, trusts are not legal entities in their own right, meaning that they can't go bankrupt or be sued. Finally, the wealth contained in a trust may accumulate with little to no taxation when trustees are based—as they often are—in one of the many low- or nil-tax jurisdictions of the former British colonies.

In addition to offering special tax and privacy protections through tools like the trust, common law provides another, more general advantage: its worldwide reach and respectability facilitate the nearly frictionless movement of capital across the globe. Because the common-law tradition spread worldwide via colonialism, asset-holding structures in one part of the system enjoy recognition and "interoperability" with legal regimes around the world. This isn't the case for some other legal systems and structures. For example, while you could enjoy some of the same tax relief and other benefits of a common-law trust by putting your wealth in a *vakf* based in a country governed by Islamic law, neither Islamic law nor the *vakf* are recognized in many other countries, creating an obstacle to moving assets internationally. While in many parts of the world a common-law trust can open a bank account and send or receive wire transfers, a *vakf* might not be granted the same international legal recognition. That's usually a deal-breaker for the ultra-wealthy, whose personal and business activities are conducted transnationally.

Widespread recognition of the trust, even in civil-law countries, is a testament to the dominance of common law and the Anglo-American role in finance and geopolitics. This is despite the fact that common law governs only about one-quarter of the 195 nations recognized by the U.N. An analogy could be made to the Linux operating system, which powers many of the world's supercomputers and forms the kernel for widely used mobile systems such as Android. Linux is "open-source," meaning that its code is open to modification by users, just as common law is to judges. Even though Linux is used by only a minority of desktop and laptop computers, its significance and global spread means that other, more widely implemented platforms (like Apple's iOS and Microsoft Windows) must provide cross-platform compatibility. Just as almost everything in computing has to interact with Linux at some level, most legal systems have to interact with the common law.

This cross-jurisdictional compatibility of common law means two very important things for the transnational super-rich. First, they know that any legal arrangements they make to protect their assets in a former British colony will likely be recognized by courts and financial institutions around the world. Second, their property will enjoy the protection and stability offered by British law, in some cases including appeals that go directly to courts in London. In the words of legal theorist Kojo Koram, many of the former colonies that evolved into offshore financial centers remain "as much British territory as Sheffield or Swansea."

From the perspective of the ultra-wealthy, putting their fortunes in trusts, corporations, and foundations based in the former British colonies is just as secure and respectable as putting them in the United Kingdom itself—but without the burdens of U.K. taxation or regulation. It is very nearly the same sweet deal the British Empire once offered to colonists: all the property and privacy protections of an advanced state system, minus most of the costs. It is one of those rare situations where it truly is possible to have your cake and eat it too.

All that said, the metamorphosis of former British colonies into the offshore financial system was ultimately an accident of history. It arose from the confluence of exogenous political change with opportunity structures the empire had already put in place—particularly the tax and legal systems described above. Leading up to and just after the Second World War, modern welfare states began to arise in North America and Europe. Big government programs, like the U.S. Social Security Administration and the U.K. National Health Service, required big tax revenues to support them. By the 1960s, the top marginal income tax rate in the United States was 91 percent. In the United Kingdom, the top rate was 95 percent, triggering protests from the country's best-known musicians: the Rolling Stones decamped across the Channel to France, and the Beatles recorded "Taxman."

Many corporations and wealthy individuals sought to avoid paying the newly hiked taxes, but they were subject to tight limitations in the form of currency controls: restrictions on the amount of a nation's money that could be transferred outside national boundaries. Until the

1970s, for example, British citizens could bring a maximum of £50 with them to pay for holiday expenses abroad—the equivalent of just over US$1,000 today. That was a significant burden, especially since credit cards weren't available to the British until 1966, about fifteen years after Americans got them. One could always risk hefty fines or even a prison term by taking suitcases full of cash to deposit in Switzerland, as British billionaire Howard Marks—an Oxford-trained nuclear physicist turned international drug lord—bragged about doing in the 1970s. But most weren't willing to take that chance.

Meanwhile, independence movements were growing in power worldwide throughout the postwar era, destabilizing all the European empires. As imperial control retreated, the colonizers' very different developmental legacies became more evident. Spain and Germany tended to colonize rich and well-populated places, then run them into the ground through brutal resource extraction, leaving little behind with which to rebuild. While the British sometimes employed a similar strategy (most infamously in India and South Africa), their empire more often targeted sparsely populated territories where the bureaucratic infrastructure of the common law could easily be transplanted, and the government administration staffed with literate and numerate natives, educated in colonial schools. The result, as one sociological study concluded, was a kind of colonization-as-cloning strategy, which turned the territories "into little Great Britains." This not only served the interests of the empire but unintentionally created the foundation for a postimperial world of self-supporting independent states, with economies based on knowledge work and expertise.

Decolonization also drove intra-imperial capital flight, from one former colony to another, seeking safe haven from political and economic turmoil. Settlers of European origin—fearful that formerly colonized subjects would impose capital controls or seize settlers' assets—often liquidated their wealth and sent it to countries that promised secrecy and security. This proved to be a boon not just for traditional "tax havens" like Switzerland (a civil-law jurisdiction popular among the French and other settlers from civil-law empires), but also for British colonies that had not yet pushed for independence. These included the Bahamas, which lagged behind other Caribbean independence movements by about a decade and so became a favored depository for the wealth of settlers in the decolonizing territories.

When these three historical events converged—decolonization, welfare state taxation, and the end of currency controls—Britain's low- and nil-tax colonies became exceptionally attractive places to park a fortune. This also presented a neat solution to the financial problem posed by decolonization. Although the British Empire began unwinding itself in 1947 by withdrawing from India, the process took another twenty-five years or so to complete, in part because it wasn't clear how many of the smaller colonies could survive economically after independence. Many, like the famously mosquito-plagued and underdeveloped Cayman Islands—long an administrative dependency of the crown colony of Jamaica—had few prospects for self-sufficiency. The Caymans had no infrastructure to support tourism (such as phone lines and widespread access to electricity) and little in the way of natural resources, subsisting instead on fishing and smallholder agriculture. Without a plan to generate revenue on their own, those territories would remain dependent on cash supports from London—a politically unpopular prospect while public services were being cut within the United Kingdom.

Building the financial sector, which required little infrastructure compared to other industries, was seen by the British government as the quickest way to develop the colonies and make them self-sufficient economically. One of the wealth managers I interviewed in Panama played a frontline role in this process. An elegant white-haired man with gracious manners and an accent straight out of Masterpiece Theatre, he was both a product of the colonial system and an instrument of its rebirth in the offshore world. Born in Rhodesia—a territory now divided between the modern African nations of Zambia and Zimbabwe—he first worked as a civil servant in the country's court system, then moved abroad to work as a trustee in the Channel Islands and Cayman Islands. After a few years in private practice, he returned to civil service to carry out a specifically imperial task. "I was sent by the British government to Turks and Caicos in 1969 to look at the financial service laws and establish a financial services commission," he recalled. "Part of my remit at that time was 'These islands are costing the British taxpayer a fortune, so we want you to encourage offshore banking and offshore corporations to develop economic independence there.'" Turks and Caicos became politically independent in the mid-1970s and now reaps 30 percent of its GDP from the financial services sector.

The basic outlines of this story were repeated throughout the retreating British Empire in the 1960s and 1970s, led by very similar characters. For example, the man behind the novel legal strategy that turned the British Virgin Islands (BVI) into the world's most popular offshore financial center was attorney Michael Riegels, born in the British East African colony of Tanganyika (now Tanzania), educated in Kenya, then admitted to the bar in the United Kingdom after taking a university degree at Oxford. After moving to the BVI, Riegels led a team of five attorneys who revolutionized the offshore world with the International Business Companies (IBC) Act: a "radical" law that created new possibilities for global tax avoidance combined with a high level of secrecy. Not only are BVI companies untaxed, they are not subject to any bookkeeping or auditing requirements. To add an extra layer of secrecy, the names of everyone involved in the company—from shareholders to directors—can be disclosed only under court order.

The legislation proved so attractive that it not only vaulted the "backwater" country to the forefront of offshore financial centers but made it rich on incorporation and registration fees. Those fees now contribute well over half of the country's national revenue. It was a stunning turnaround for a place that had been written off a generation earlier by a seasoned imperial administrator, who wrote in 1947, "There is no more backward unit in the British Colonial Empire." The country now hosts about 40 percent of the global offshore financial services business, representing hundreds of billions of dollars in corporate and private wealth. British Virgin Islanders are said to "enjoy a standard of living far higher than on other Caribbean islands." As a result of this transformation, the IBC Act attained the status of a "quasi-religious text" in the postcolonial world. Other aspiring financial centers copied it so widely—often verbatim, changing only the name of the jurisdiction—that *all* offshore companies, no matter where they were based, became known internationally for a time as "BVIs."

An even more startling transformation occurred in the Cayman Islands. There, attorney William Walker—born in the South American colony of British Guiana (now the independent country of Guyana), educated in the colony of Barbados and then at Cambridge—designed the Trust Law, Companies Law, and other legal infrastructure that turned the islands into one of the world's leading tax havens. Within twenty years, the Caymans went from a poor and unwanted dependency of Jamaica to the country with the Caribbean's highest levels of personal wealth, boasting a per capita income higher than that of Great

Britain itself. For performing this "economic miracle," Queen Elizabeth II made Walker an Officer of the Order of the British Empire (OBE).

While I never got the chance to speak with Walker, I did interview one of his main collaborators in creating the Caymans as an offshore center: the distinguished British barrister Milton Grundy, recently eulogized in the London newspapers as "the éminence grise" of offshore finance. In a phone call conducted in 2019, Grundy (who died four years later at ninety-six) described how the rise of new financial centers was driven by racialized fear of postcolonial independence movements and anticipated reprisals against the white elite. "I did a lot of work in the Caribbean at that time, mostly in the Bahamas," he said, recalling the late 1960s. "There was a lot of political uncertainty, because power was moving from white people to black people, so wealthy people wanted to get their money out. People were looking to the Caymans as an escape, because the governor was white, and there was no political agitation." When Jamaica declared independence in 1962, the Caymans went in the opposite direction, opting to come under direct British rule. Shortly thereafter, the governor of the Caymans asked Grundy to write new financial laws, triggering an avalanche of incoming settler cash. The result, as one London-based journalist put it, was "the most notorious tax haven on Earth, but . . . more British than Britain."

Transforming the rest of the former colonies into fiscal paradises seemed like a win-win solution: the colonies could support themselves with fees from financial services, and the imperial metropole could get the territories "off the payroll." Behind the scenes, however, this strategy provoked a years-long struggle within the imperial administration and the British civil service. On one side was the British Treasury, which argued that a low- or nil-tax regime was unsustainable for countries seeking independence. On the other side was the Bank of

England and the Foreign and Commonwealth Office, both of which saw the tax-haven plan "as a means for territories to 'pay their own way' and not drain Britain's economy." By the mid-1970s, the latter group had won out—supported by settler elites who wished to remain as lightly taxed as possible—leading to the efflorescence in the global political economy that we now call the offshore financial system.

Against that historical backdrop, let us return to the story of the Bahamas, and its metamorphosis from economic backwater to power-house of global finance. European colonization on a global scale argu-ably started in the Bahamas: in 1492, the very first people Christopher Columbus encountered in the Americas were the Indigenous Lucayans on what is now known as the island of Grand Bahama, the northern-most part of the archipelago. When Ponce de León arrived twenty-one years later, the Lucayans were gone, having been kidnapped by Spanish slave traders. For centuries afterward, "pirates . . . made the Bahamas their base and were the *de facto* rulers." Well into the twentieth century, the islands were still considered "primitive and rustic," populated by a small white elite governing the descendants of enslaved people: those who had worked plantations established by the British, as well as by pro-monarchy and pro-Confederacy Americans who'd fled there fol-lowing the revolution of 1776 and the Civil War.

But while that native-born population eked out a subsistence liv-ing, the Bahamas grew to occupy an important liminal space in the global commercial network: a place where the laws didn't apply and fortunes could be made. Since the seventeenth-century heyday of com-petitive imperialism in the Caribbean region, the Bahamas had served as a free port, where mercantilist restrictions on trade were suspended. In many ways, what the Bahamas became in the twentieth century was just a reboot of what it had been centuries earlier for traders from the

British, French, Spanish, and Dutch empires in the colonial Caribbean. It was one of the key places where all four imperial powers could meet and enrich one another through trade that would otherwise have been illegal. Under mercantilist policy, colonial trade was limited to an empire's own ships and its own ports. But since the Spanish and others desperately needed manufactured goods from Britain, and could pay in Mexican silver, the four European nations carved out a handful of trading posts where laws and taxation were suspended.

The benefits of being a law-free zone intermittently boosted the economy of the Bahamas from the age of piracy through the early twentieth century, when two changes on the North American mainland triggered a much steadier flow of cash to the islands. First, Canadians discovered that they could avoid all income tax back home by residing in the Bahamas for six months or more—thanks to an agreement linking the two countries in the British Commonwealth. Second, Americans experienced Prohibition (in which the 18th Amendment prohibited the sale or import of alcoholic beverages) followed by the New Deal, which raised taxes on the rich. This created what social scientists call a "criminogenic environment"—one that increased the economic incentives to commit illegal acts, such as bootlegging alcohol to Americans and helping them evade taxes. Shady operators called it a golden opportunity.

Located just fifty-three miles from Miami Beach—the distance of a day sail—the Bahamas makes for a convenient spot to engage in activities that aren't permitted under U.S. law. In the 1860s, Nassau grew rich for a few years by helping the Confederacy evade the Union's maritime blockade, becoming a trading post where Southern cotton was exchanged for British arms. When, in 1920, Prohibition banned the sale of liquor on American soil, the islands became a hub of "rum-running." This turned out to be what local historians have described as a "godsend for the Bahamian economy," creating a steady flow of income from wealthy tourists and buyers, to supplement a "desperately poor" nation just getting by on fishing and agriculture.

In an echo of the seventeenth-century era of pirate nests and colonial free ports, enterprising Americans like William McCoy made fortunes for themselves, too. They'd sail to Nassau (where liquor sales were legal under British law), buy gin and whiskey by the case, then resell them to Americans while moored in international waters three miles off the U.S. East Coast. Setting a precedent for the workings of offshore finance, where "creative compliance" is standard practice, McCoy's business model obeyed the letter of U.S. law while violating it in spirit. Because he never sold liquor in U.S. territory, his trade was formally legal. And, legend has it, because he earned a reputation for selling undiluted, full-strength products, his name became a byword for authenticity: "the real McCoy."

This tradition of using the Bahamas to skirt the laws of other countries continued in the mid-1930s, when Americans started moving to the islands to escape the increased taxes imposed by Franklin Roosevelt's New Deal. That's what led Wallace Groves—an American financier who later turned the Bahamas into a world-leading offshore financial center—to visit the islands on his yacht and pioneer the offshore tax-evasion schemes that later earned him a two-year federal prison sentence. Groves and other tax dodgers from North America and Europe were drawn to the Bahamas not only for the lack of financial regulation but for the promise of secrecy and stability offered by the institutions of British imperialism.

Because of laws designed as an "imperial perk" for white settlers, the Bahamas levied no taxes on personal or corporate income. It did business in English—a major attraction for North Americans—and was governed by English law; the ultimate court of appeal for disputes in the Bahamas was the Privy Council in London. And since the colonial Bahamas was part of the sterling area, meaning that its currency was the British pound, its economy was tied to the stabilizing force of monetary governance based at the Bank of England. But the cherry on the sundae for wealthy foreigners was the security of knowing that what happened in Nassau would stay in Nassau. As one native Bahamian historian, Anthony Audley Thompson, described the country's appeal to people like Groves:

> Another factor was the secrecy accorded their [companies'] operations. Many of these companies were in effect legal fictions designed solely for the purpose of evading taxation in countries abroad. Because no treaties provided for the exchange of financial information between the Bahamas and other governments, the accounts of such corporations were not subject to scrutiny by foreign authorities. Nor did the Bahamas Government require financial statements to be filed by these largely imaginary holding companies.

In short, the British colonial administration had unintentionally put in place the essential legal and financial infrastructure necessary to build an ideal offshore financial center: one that catered to the libertarian ideal that rejected regulation and conceptualized the only proper function of the state as protection of private property. The only thing missing was the creative insight to realize that those colonial elements could be reconfigured for the benefit of people who weren't settlers and might never set foot on the islands at all.

After serving his time in a U.S. federal penitentiary, Groves relocated permanently to Grand Bahama in the mid-1940s and got to work recolonizing it—not in the name of any country's empire but for the benefit of himself and a multinational oligarchy. Martinican poet and politician Aimé Césaire soon recognized the shadow that figures like Groves were casting on the Caribbean, noting that in the project of colonization and its aftermath, "the decisive actors are the adventurer and the pirate." In keeping with this pattern, Groves was assisted by other denizens of the international financial demimonde, including a Canadian gambler and Mafia associate, as well as a former Swiss banker who had escaped the French penal colony of Devil's Island (the prison settlement immortalized in the Steve McQueen film *Papillon*) after his own conviction for financial crimes. Eventually, organized crime moved in via Groves's "silent partner" Meyer Lansky, one of the twentieth century's most feared and powerful mobsters.

The pivotal moment in Groves's project was the creation of the special zone he carved out on the island of Grand Bahama, dubbed Freeport. In what historians of the Bahamas have called a "surrender of sovereignty"—a defining event in colonization processes throughout history—the country's government handed over fifty thousand acres of land (about 15 percent of the island's total landmass) for Groves to own and administer personally, free of taxation and regulation for ninety-nine years. Formalized in the Hawksbill Creek Agreement of 1955, the deal gave Groves broad authority to administer police payrolls and expel "undesirables." As an exposé in *Life* magazine noted, with "the authority of a feudal baron he distributes privileges and business licenses—and when the whimsy serves him, he takes them away." The arrangement thus bore some similarities to the British colonization of Hong Kong—another time-limited agreement that triggered the metamorphosis of a strategic international trading post into a leading offshore financial center.

The key distinction was that in the Bahamas, Groves himself was acting as the colonizing power on behalf of a multinational elite, *inside* British imperial territory. He'd created a colony within a colony. His project was thus a twentieth-century update on the much older tradition of "empire by private contract," in which rogues and adventurers from around the British Empire would claim a swath of sovereign land via treaties of dubious legality, then declare themselves absolute rulers. True to type, Groves acquired land in Grand Bahama through a series of shady deals, including one based on the forged will of a blind, illiterate native farmer.

The Hawksbill Creek Agreement formalized Groves's acquisition-by-dispossession strategy and gave it the state's seal of approval. *Life* likened the arrangement to the "blank-check" charters given in 1600 by Queen Elizabeth I to the British East India Company—the catalyst for a centuries-long enterprise of plunder and pillage that brought a globe-spanning empire into being. Groves's innovation, such as it was, lay in bringing a practice imposed on distant lands in Southeast Asia and Africa right to the backyard of the twentieth-century United States. That included the racialized oppression and violence that underpinned the whole enterprise, leading the *New York Times* to compare Nassau under Groves not only to a monarchy but to a "police-state" polity.

Groves's arrangement wasn't simply an *imitation* of old colonial practices: it was directly dependent on the then-current colonial infrastructure. As the historians of the Grand Bahama Museum—an organization founded and managed by the Groves family—have acknowledged of the Hawksbill Creek Agreement, "This remarkable contract between the Bahamian colonial government and a private corporation wholly owned by the Groves family was negotiated at a time when the old colonial structure was still in place." This meant that the new empire of offshore finance was literally built atop the older structures of British imperialism, just as the Spanish built their colonial structures directly atop the main institutions of their imperial predecessors, the Incas.

Within fifteen years of the agreement, Groves's creation was flourishing to such an extent that the *Economist* described the Bahamas as "the archetype of the tax haven." Local publications billed it as the "Little Switzerland of the Western Hemisphere." Hundreds of American, Canadian, and Swiss banks opened branches in the capital city of Nassau, and the offshore business employed nearly 10 percent of the island's population—an estimated 85 percent of whom were Black Bahamians.

The influx of money meant that the transport and telecommunications infrastructure of Nassau and Freeport became comparable to those available in the United States. This allowed the Bahamas to claim credibly that it was a hub of transnational capital, firmly embedded in the global network of offshore financial centers and former British colonies. At the same time, there was growing competition from the up-and-coming Cayman Islands and other imperial territories. Thus, two years after Bahamians declared independence from the British, an interview with the governor of the Central Bank concluded that "national self-sufficiency and self-reliance" required that the country not only continue its practices but also aggressively expand its role as an offshore financial center.

What this meant in practice was acknowledged as unsavory, even in the Bahamian press. One Bahamian accountant wrote bluntly of how wealthy foreigners availed themselves of the opportunities the islands offered for legal legerdemain:

Some of the methods employed by foreigners utilizing the Bahamas are:

1. Opening up secret bank accounts;
2. Purchasing shell companies for given transactions;
3. Interposing unrelated third parties (in the Bahamas), usually on a commission basis, for terminal tax-avoidance purposes; and
4. Fabrication of pre-dated agreements, commitments, invoices, etc., to accommodate income diversion to the Bahamas.

. . . At best, most are on the fringe of the laws of the high-tax country being deprived of the income and thus, give rise to questions of morality.

The implications were clear: the Bahamas would sustain postcolonial fiscal independence by helping wealthy foreigners break their own countries' laws. The Bahamian government explicitly gave state sanction to fabrication and fraud. Groves had re-created the seventeenth-century pirate nest with all the modern conveniences.

As a "freelance imperialist," Groves—like his buccaneer predecessors—acted not on behalf of any nation but on behalf of capital. He pushed and bent the boundaries of the law as far as he could until someone stopped him, which wasn't very often because he was making so many powerful people fabulously rich. He succeeded to such a remarkable degree that in 2019, the *Financial Times* described the Bahamas as "the richest country in the Caribbean" in terms of GDP per capita, due largely to its offshore financial services business, which by then made up an estimated 20 percent of its national economy. These figures represent an extraordinary transformation from the Bahamas of the mid-1940s, when local historians recorded widespread destitution and occasional death by starvation. This extreme economic vulnerability made the Bahamas ripe for get-rich-quick operators like Groves—a pattern of predation observed throughout the postcolonial states in the 1960s and 1970s.

The genuinely dire straits in which most Bahamians lived prior to Groves's arrival may account for the near-hagiographic treatment of him decades later, even by the native Black elite. In an obsequious essay published to commemorate the tenth anniversary of the Hawksbill Creek Agreement, the Black editor-publisher of *The Bahamian Review* magazine praised "intrepid developer Wallace Groves" and "the invaluable service done to this section of Mankind by the creator of Freeport." This language is of a piece with the god-king image many ultra-wealthy clients of offshore finance cultivate for themselves. In fact, by the late 1960s, the American press had literally dubbed Groves "King of the Bahamas."

But even as the islands' national wealth increased, inequality skyrocketed. The result has been a landscape of poverty punctuated by a series of "tremendously wealthy private empires" owned and operated by a few white men like Groves and his cronies. Groves ticked all the same boxes as nineteenth-century buccaneer Sir James Brooke, who subdued the Malaysian island of Borneo with the help of the British imperial fleet, then carved out a bit for his own private use, declaring himself king in 1841. Soon afterward, he was knighted in London and made governor of another territory on Borneo: Labuan, now an offshore financial center in its own right. Like Brooke, Groves was a specialist in plunder who established a colony within a colony, repurposed imperial institutions for private benefit, then accumulated wealth through dispossession, enforced by authoritarian white supremacy. In that one sentence is the "recipe" for creating an offshore financial center.

CHAPTER 4

The Paradox of Plenty

I N THE EARLY 1990S, ECONOMIC geographers and political scientists coined the term "resource curse" to describe a paradox they observed in countries where valuable natural resources were discovered: rather than thriving, such countries often crumbled, economically and politically. Instead of raising living standards for all, the newfound wealth generated violence, inequality, and corruption. Terry Karl, a Stanford political science professor, dubbed this phenomenon the "paradox of plenty." She discerned the pattern all over the world, from Venezuela (where she did her research on the destruction wrought by oil wealth) to Sierra Leone (home of blood diamonds) and Afghanistan (which, despite its estimated $3 trillion in mineral wealth, remains among the poorest and most corrupt countries in the world).

The paradox has also arisen in most of the world's offshore financial centers. Like the countries affected by the resource curse, many offshore centers are former colonial states struggling to stay fiscally viable. Their resource is human capital: a population literate and numerate enough to perform the filing and compliance tasks required to service offshore corporations, trusts, and foundations. For these economically and politically fragile countries, the influx of cash provided by international finance seems like an unmitigated blessing, offering jobs and revenues for a relatively small investment in infrastructure. Just some office space with computers and high-speed internet access, and they're in business.

But becoming an offshore financial center has unexpected costs. Precipitous economic, political, and social declines have occurred so often in such states that observers have coined a new term for it: the "finance curse," a subtype of the paradox of plenty. When the finance curse strikes, a recurrent pattern unfolds. While a stricken country's democracy, economy, and culture remain formally intact, they are increasingly oriented to and co-opted by international elites. Such nations gradually become organized around the interests of people who don't even live there, to the detriment of those who do. As legal scholar Kojo Koram has noted, under such conditions local representative democracy becomes performative at best, and divorced from authentic popular sovereignty. "Despite the appearance that decisions are being made by elected politicians," he writes, "the network of tax havens weakens the ability of democratic actors to take any decisions that would harm the financial markets."

Scratch the surface of a fiscal paradise and you'll usually find a captured state. High-net-worth individuals, multinational firms, and finance professionals from abroad not only wrest disproportionate benefits from the country's economy but exert undue influence over its political system as well. While many studies have pointed out how offshore financial centers damage *other* countries—by destroying onshore tax bases and undermining their democracies—far less attention has been paid to the damage the offshore financial services business inflicts on its hosts. That's because the locals who bear the brunt of the damage are rarely heard from in international discourse.

While becoming an offshore center is usually touted as a development strategy that produces economic miracles for poor countries, the benefits are often illusory or short-lived. It's not just that the riches seldom trickle down to locals in offshore centers: the attention and resources of their governments are diverted to serve the interests of the ultra-wealthy living abroad. This leads to increasing economic *and* social fragility, along with political corruption, in many offshore financial centers. "Those in power battle to control money flows rather than serve the public," as British journalist Oliver Bullough put it recently.

One result of this local decay and neglect is the escalation of crime and violence. These characteristic consequences of the finance curse began to intersect with my own research as offshore data-gathering trips took me farther and farther away from the offshore industry's urban metropoles in Europe and North America. In the elegantly appointed wealth management offices of Zurich and London, the menace of offshore finance is well hidden beneath bespoke suits and formal good manners. But in the smaller and often remote countries most dependent on offshore finance—the "secrecy plantations" where the cash crops of confidentiality and impunity are really produced—the veneer of politesse is much thinner. There's less demand for it, since wealthy international clients rarely visit. There, I began to encounter some of the hostility and threats that others, including natives who challenge the offshore system, have experienced.

In retrospect, it's not wholly surprising that some people working in the offshore financial services industry might want for themselves a bit of the lawlessness they produce for sale to their elite clientele. This aspirational impunity—a political force I think is woefully underestimated—manifests in a variety of ways, from abuse of the law to harass those investigating the offshore centers, to physical violence and other forms of criminality. Of course, versions of this phenomenon arise in many countries, not just offshore centers. When the most powerful members of a society flaunt their impunity, it becomes a kind of status symbol for their followers, whose imitative disregard for the law can take many destructive forms. Though crime exists everywhere, the offshore centers are distinguished by the perceptions of some locals that the *offshore finance industry itself has made the problem significantly worse.*

Whistleblowers and journalists—particularly women—have paid far higher prices than I did for inquiring into that industry and its connections to the powerful. One former wealth manager turned whistleblower told a reporter that she could never return to her former home in the Bahamas after "breaking the private bankers' code of silence," saying, "I don't want to have concrete shoes put on me." Perhaps as a warning to would-be whistleblowers, or just to reassure clients who might be up to no good, some offshore private banks, law firms, and wealth managers cultivate an image of ruthlessness and even implied violence beneath the veneer of upper-crust service. For example, the well-established Bahamian firm Harry B. Sands, Lobosky & Company advertises itself as "relentless," "famously formidable," and "feared by their adversaries." The founder himself is described as a "crack shot" and "an iron hand in a velvet glove"—phrases seemingly more suited to a *Godfather* film than to a professional services firm.

Former Swiss banker turned whistleblower Rudolf Elmer made the implied connection explicit, comparing the offshore financial services industry to "the mafia." Elmer, who had been the chief operating and compliance officer in the Cayman Islands for Zurich-based private bank Julius Bär, said he tried for years to raise the alarm in the Swiss legal system and media about the tax evasion and other abuses of offshore secrecy that he'd witnessed. "It is damaging our society," Elmer said in a 2011 press conference. "I wanted to let society know what I know." After turning whistleblower in 2008 by sharing incriminating bank documents with WikiLeaks, Elmer claimed that he, his wife, and their young child were stalked and harassed for years by henchmen working for Julius Bär. At one point, he received an email traced to a public internet terminal near his home; the message read, "We are here. Your daughter will be killed if you do not stop." The bank denied any involvement in these activities but acknowledged that it spent more than one million Swiss francs (roughly US$1.1 million) surveilling Elmer's activities.

Reporter Daphne Caruana Galizia paid with her life for publishing exposés on the criminal activities connected to offshore finance in her native Malta. She led local investigations into Maltese officials exposed in the Panama Papers, implicating the country's then prime minister as well as his political rivals in money laundering. They had been taking kickbacks and hiding the proceeds via secret accounts in other offshore centers. While Malta had long been known as an outpost of smugglers and pirates, the country's emergence as an offshore financial center supercharged the lawlessness. As one longtime Maltese political operative and journalist put it, criminality is now "perpetrated by the state. It's not just sanctioned by the state."

Caruana Galizia was assassinated by a car bomb in October 2017, just minutes after posting to her blog that "there are crooks everywhere you look now. The situation is desperate." After two of his close aides were implicated in the murder, the prime minister resigned. Older Maltese interviewed in the aftermath of Caruana Galizia's death expressed shock at how quickly their country had changed. One retiree told the

Economist, "You expect something like this to happen over there"—pointing toward Mafia-dominated Sicily, visible about fifty nautical miles in the distance—"but not here."

In my decades of working life, only my research on the offshore financial system has come with legal and physical threats. None of the other work I've done has brought the slightest hint of danger, including the couple of years I spent as a young reporter for the Associated Press and *Newsweek* before going to graduate school. Though I was often assigned to interview potentially dangerous people, including members of the Ku Klux Klan and drunk fans in sports bars during the World Series, none of them ever menaced me.

But once I got into the "deep end" of offshore, the risks associated with investigating the pervasive lawlessness and corruption created by the finance curse became palpable. Most striking was the passivity, or sometimes active complicity, of the government. Unlike the corrupt bureaucrats one might encounter elsewhere, offshore officials are engaged in the seemingly paradoxical effort to protect their countries' international reputation at all costs (to attract foreign investors and depositors) while at the same time countenancing many forms of local lawlessness. Police officers and political leaders I encountered seemed both helpless and cynical, effectively taking a "Forget it, Jake, it's Chinatown" view of their work. Their withdrawal from conflict created a power vacuum that criminals and petty tyrants rushed to fill.

That is how I came to contemplate jumping out of a moving taxi in the middle of sugarcane fields on a moonless night while doing research on the Indian Ocean island of Mauritius. I was heading back to my hotel after interviewing a Mauritian wealth manager. After warning me that crime was on the rise, the wealth manager sent me off in a taxi, escorted by a minor government official who was to ensure my safety on the thirty-minute journey. That was a first for me, but it seemed like a well-intentioned gesture.

At the outset of the trip, the driver made small talk in English about the weather, then noted that it was the one-year anniversary of the murder of a female tourist on the island—an Irishwoman who had been on her honeymoon, killed at the hotel where I was staying by a thief she surprised mid-robbery. This was news to me. While I was taking it in, the driver pivoted to asking me what *I* was doing in Mauritius. When I told him I was looking into the offshore finance industry, he turned to me with a broad smile and said, "Government don't want you here, won't help you." It was such an unexpected comment that I just sat there in silent confusion. It seemed particularly strange that my escort said nothing. Instead, he looked at the taxi driver and laughed. They seemed to know each other.

Within a few minutes, we were on an unlit two-lane road through sugarcane fields, with no other cars or buildings or lights in sight. The taxi driver put his hand on my right thigh and squeezed. (I was sitting up front with him because there was more legroom for my nearly six-foot frame.) My escort, sitting behind me, put his hand on my shoulder and fiddled with my bra strap. I froze in shock, then considered my odds of surviving a two-to-one fight or a leap onto the hard pavement. Meanwhile, they kept talking to each other and laughing, as casual and confident as if they were probing the fruit at a market stall.

What alarmed me most was their carefree cockiness, as if being held accountable was simply outside the realm of possibility. That sent my mind racing back to what I'd read about the island in preparation for my visit: the rule of law was in tatters, with the former finance minister under arrest for graft and thousands marching in the streets against rampant corruption. Not an ideal environment for seeking justice, especially for a pesky foreigner asking inconvenient questions about a mainstay of the country's economy. In that context, the two men having a little "fun" with me would have had little to fear from law enforcement. The authorities might well decide that I "had it coming" due to the negative exposure my research could bring to Mauritius. In fact, shortly after I left the island, the U.S. Department of State flagged Mauritius for its human rights abuses: government officials were using the police to harass and unlawfully jail foreign journalists investigating financial crimes. The country had a lot to lose from inquisitive outsiders.

I'll never know for sure what was in store for me that night, because I lucked out: lights unexpectedly appeared ahead of us on the otherwise dark, empty road. There had been an accident, creating a cluster of cars and a bit of traffic. Suddenly, there were people around, in nearby cars and standing along the roadside. One woman bystander looked into the taxi and started yelling; she ran after us and managed to land a blow on the taxi's rear window before the driver sped up and away. But by far the most surprising development was the behavior of the government official, who instantly withdrew his hand from me and shrank down in his seat, while the laughing taxi driver said, "To transank! To transank!" I later learned that this was Mauritian Creole for "your girlfriend." Apparently, she gave the government official more to worry about than the police. In any case, the men kept their hands to themselves for the last few minutes of the ride, until we reached my hotel. To my relief, I never saw either of them again during my brief remaining time on the island.

Mauritius is in many ways a poster child for the finance curse: a struggling agrarian nation after gaining independence from Britain in 1968, it entered the financial services industry in the 1990s and was transformed from one of the poorest countries in Africa to one of the richest. Enough of that wealth came from shady or outright illegal sources that, within three years of my fieldwork there, Mauritius made the European Commission's top thirty blacklist of offshore centers, as well as Oxfam's top fifteen list of the world's most destructive tax havens, based on the country's failure to cooperate with other countries in stemming financial crime. Shortly afterward, several top government ministers were found to have welcomed drug-trafficking money to Mauritius, boosting the country's offshore financial services industry and pocketing a hefty sum for themselves. After the Paradise Papers revealed that Mauritius was home to half a million secret companies established by one law firm alone, a third-generation sugar farmer told the International Consortium of Investigative Journalists that "the Mauritius government has abandoned" the country's native workers in favor of the financial services industry. They had also abandoned much of the law.

About eighteen months later, I encountered a different face of the finance curse on the other side of the world, in the British Virgin Islands. The country had been transformed in "paradox of plenty" style by wealth managers who bent its nascent democracy to serve the needs of international private wealth. The innovative and widely copied International Business Companies Act of 1984 was rubber-stamped by the BVI legislature, without any public debate or any chance of opposition by local voters. Within a decade, the country was awash in foreign cash escaping onshore tax and regulation through BVI incorporation. With so many "businessmen" arriving with suitcases full of banknotes, BVI bankers complained that their cash-counting machines were breaking down from overuse.

But the wealth generated by the four hundred thousand companies and their $1.5 trillion in assets has not yielded much benefit for the majority of the islands' populace. With corporate and individual income taxes abolished in 2004 to make the BVI even more attractive to foreign capital, locals carry most of the fiscal burden of the state. A hefty 8 percent payroll tax is docked from their paychecks, plus another 4 percent in Social Security contributions. In contrast, Americans pay 7.65 percent in *combined* payroll and Social Security levies. This means the working people of the BVI face a regressive tax at 157 percent the rate paid by their counterparts in the United States.

Moreover, the islands have descended into such corruption that an independent commission—headed by a retired British judge—was appointed to investigate BVI government officials. The commission's report not only documented the officials' involvement in drug and financial crimes but showed that they were engaged in campaigns of intimidation against journalists and community leaders looking into those activities. The basic outlines of the story were nearly identical to those of finance-cursed Mauritius. The commission concluded its report in 2021 by observing that, in the BVI, "the principles of good governance, such as openness, transparency and even the rule of law, are ignored." A year after the report was published, the head of government, Premier Andrew Fahie, was revealed to be running a lucrative cocaine-trafficking and money-laundering operation.

This information wasn't available in August 2013 when I arrived to interview a group of wealth managers in the capital city of Road Town. So I was taken aback when the first participant I met—a sixty-something Englishman—greeted me with crossed arms, a hostile glare, and a threat to have me deported. That was a first: typically, off-shore professionals who felt as he did simply refused my request for an interview. Those who did agree to sit with me usually wanted to manage impressions in a positive way.

Instead, he accused me of committing a kind of "thought crime" against his profession, saying he'd Googled my work and found it to be "left-leaning" and "disapproving of what the [wealth management] industry and wealthy people are doing." Baffled, I asked him what he was talking about. It turned out his internet search on me had yielded the one and only article I'd produced at that point in my project, published in a relatively little-read academic journal. His objection? That the article's *subtitle* included the word "Inequality."

To me, it seemed factually indisputable that offshore finance helped the rich get richer. The article mustered a raft of economic data to illustrate that point. But as this man made clear, he wasn't challenging the evidence: "inequality" all by itself was a fighting word. He alluded ominously to the anger of the local wealth management community, several of whose members I was scheduled to interview in the coming days. The implication seemed to be that if I displeased him further, his colleagues might cancel on me. Rather than argue with him, I tried to redirect his attention to my interview questions about his career trajectory. After answering in a calm and measured fashion, he surprised me by revving up into anger again, concluding our appointment with a diatribe about the ways professionals like him had been "vilified" for being "immoral." A colleague had told him, he said with relish, that, because of my "agenda," I "should be thrown off the island."

The last part was so bizarre that I wondered briefly if the man might be in the grips of psychological distress, a momentary break from reality. After all, deportation is a decision to be made by governments, not accountants and bankers. I was tempted to press him for more details about throwing me off the island, but the hostility and agitation of his body language gave me pause. I had the impression of being baited into a show of alarm or defensiveness by someone looking for a pretext to lash out. So I did what many women do when confronted by men who appear irrationally angry and spoiling for a fight: I smiled and nodded and made myself as emotionally blank as possible, while heading expeditiously for the door. Back at my hotel, I made a beeline for the bar and immediately ordered a stiff drink. I was shaking.

About halfway through my cocktail, I calmed down enough to wonder: *Had* anyone ever been deported for getting on the wrong side of offshore wealth managers? A few seconds on Google brought me to the story of Leah McGrath Goodman, a former *Newsweek* journalist who had in fact been deported from the Channel Island tax haven of Jersey after investigating illegal activity there. Not only that, but she'd been interrogated at Heathrow Airport for hours afterward by British immigration officials. Because the Channel Islands are part of the British Common Travel Area (along with the Isle of Man and Ireland), the border agents were authorized to prevent Goodman from entering the whole area—which they did, imposing a travel ban of two years. But the offense was difficult to understand, because Goodman wasn't writing about finance at all. She was investigating allegations of sexual abuse at a children's care home on the island: Haut de la Garenne, later dubbed the "house of horror" by the British media.

As later reporting by others revealed, Jersey's financial services professionals had for years acted to suppress the Haut de la Garenne story, apparently out of concern that the negative publicity would threaten the island's reputation as a quiet, respectable place for international elites to park their wealth. That reputation was already in some peril. Other journalists had begun to publicize the crippling of Jersey's economy, government, and society by the offshore financial services industry. Once considered a "miracle of plenty" and a role model for other would-be tax havens, it had become a textbook tragedy of the finance curse. Unlike Goodman, however, most of the journalists behind those investigations were U.K. citizens and thus not subject to the kind of border-control harassment she experienced.

Still, the island's wealth management industry went to extraordinary lengths to suppress the "house of horrors" investigation. Jersey's own chief of police claimed he'd been suspended in 2008 at the behest of the island's financial services elites for pursuing the child abuse case; he told reporters that his work threatened the island's carefully cultivated "secrecy culture." Similarly, Jersey's former health minister claimed that he'd been fired for pursuing the abuse investigation. In 2009, he fled to London seeking political asylum (which he received). By the time Goodman came along in 2011, the financial elites had extended their influence to border enforcement in the United Kingdom, an effort apparently supported by sympathetic London-based financiers eager to protect their own business on the island. It took intervention from Parliament to restore Goodman's right to enter the United Kingdom.

After this unexpectedly sobering read, I realized that the threat from the BVI banker was credible and that my experience in Mauritius wasn't a one-off unpleasantness. Both incidents now appeared in a new light, as glancing encounters with something systemic and troubling. Naturally, I wanted to know more about it.

Just two years later, I had another brush with the finance curse, this time in the Cook Islands—an idyllic South Pacific archipelago famous for its unique contribution to the offshore world in the form of the impenetrable asset-protection trust. A thief broke into the room at Pae Moana while I was asleep with my young child, approaching so close that the intruder's heavy breathing woke me. As I popped up out of bed, the intruder fled—taking my smartphone, which was my only means of communication with the outside world, thanks to the local SIM card I'd purchased a few hours earlier. We were fine physically, but I had nightmares about the incident for years afterward. When I made my police report, the officer told us this sort of crime happened with some frequency, particularly there on the main island, where the wealth management offices were located.

Though I tried desperately to get us onto the next flight home, it was impossible: the few flights to the United States were booked for days to come. We could have flown to New Zealand, but it was several thousand miles in the wrong direction, and I was on a tight research budget. It was barely possible to make calls, not only because my own phone was gone but because telecommunications infrastructure on the island was very limited. Even in the capital, it was impossible then to get internet access or an international phone line without a calling card purchased from one of the local telecom providers—which were open for only a few hours on weekdays—or via guest access at one of the major resorts. We were effectively trapped by the extreme isolation that was such an asset for the Cook Islands as an offshore center.

After finishing with the police and giving up on getting us an outbound flight, I took my son for a walk. We ended up at a small harbor where a Maori fisherman was cleaning his catch: a mahi-mahi. It's such a wonderfully strange-looking fish that I stopped and stared like a child at the iridescent green skin and huge squared-off fore-head. I must have appeared as dazed and traumatized as I felt, because the fisherman looked up from his work to ask me what was wrong. When I explained, he laughed bitterly and said he'd heard such stories before; to my surprise, he added that crime rates on the island had shot up since the financial services industry had grown so powerful. The way he described the past few decades, it was as if being in the business of evading the law had created a kind of contagion, corrupting even aspects of island life that had nothing to do with finance. "Everyone calls us the Crook Islands now," he said. From the

Indigenous hospitality traditions to the nation's democratic institutions, he added, the finance industry had corroded everything. Referring to a recent political-corruption scandal, the fisherman concluded, "They've got our government in their pockets. I hate what they've done to my country."

The point of this story isn't that crime or corruption exists in the Cook Islands but that a person who'd lived there all his life had noticed both a qualitative and a quantitative shift for the worse as a result of the country becoming part of the offshore financial system. Remoteness made places like the Cook Islands among the most productive "secrecy plantations," where investigators from abroad rarely ventured and there was no need for the veneer of law-abiding respectability one encounters in Zurich, London, and New York. Out there in the peripheral fiscal paradises, where the most important work in the system gets done, a certain disregard for the niceties of "law and order" seemed to take hold, assisted by the benign neglect of local authorities. All that seemed to matter was keeping the financial services industry and its clients happy.

The Cook Islands experience really brought home to me how much geography still matters despite the hypermobility of people and capital. Tiny as it is, the country's remoteness constitutes a veritable superpower: the ability to ignore and defy the wishes of much larger and richer countries. Panama, a former colony of Spain and the United States, employs a similar strategy as the Cook Islands, with similar results for the country's financial services industry. While Panama isn't remote, it is small: a narrow, S-shaped strip of land occupying less space than the state of South Carolina. But because it sits on a geographical choke point in the global economy, the Panama Canal, the country has withstood decades of international pressure to curtail its involvement in the offshore financial services business. A wealth manager I interviewed there explained:

> The OECD threatens to blacklist countries that don't share tax information, but . . . Panama has leverage. It has something called the Retaliation Act—allowing the country to use economic leverage to fight back against attacks. In practice, that means shutting down the canal. This is especially important with the U.S., which has had a Big Brother relationship with Panama for more than a century. So Panama has a credible threat to use against strong-arming from the OECD and America: the country can shut down the economy of the U.S. East Coast if they want.

This way of reframing Panama's offshore financial services business as a form of postcolonial resistance also recasts any regulatory effort from the international community as "economic imperialism." I encountered this rationale elsewhere in my journey around the offshore world, and other scholars—like political scientist Jason Sharman—have written whole books about it. To be sure, the offshore financial services industry allowed former colonies to turn the tables, enabling them to exploit the colonial metropoles by draining their wealth and undermining their laws. But what might have been a "revenge of the colonized" story doesn't have such a satisfying conclusion: instead, the former colonies end up selling impunity to global elites while offloading the costs of society onto their own local populations.

The Panama Papers leak of 2016 unfolded against this postcolonial history. When forty years' worth of confidential client data from the Panama City–based wealth management law firm Mossack Fonseca became public, the tabloid-like headlines focused on the lifestyles of the rich and famous: the celebrities, heads of state, and corporate leaders who used Panama to enjoy the benefits of society without paying the costs. But the effects on Panama itself were largely overlooked.

When I went there in 2013 to conduct research, one of the native Panamanian wealth managers I interviewed said that he always reminded his billionaire clients that there were people living in cardboard boxes under bridges not two miles from where they sat, and maybe they should think about addressing that problem. "They don't like it, but they haven't fired me yet," he added with a grin. I saw a little of the brutal poverty he was talking about as I traveled through Panama City. The contrast between the shiny office towers of the business district and the squalor of neighborhoods across town, like El Chorrillo—where many native Panamanians said they feared to go—was vertiginous.

Latin America leads the world in wealth inequality, and Panama is among the most unequal nations in the region—second only to Brazil. Its economy has been booming throughout the twenty-first century, but its poverty rate has grown to over 20 percent. The financial services industry catering to foreigners contributes a healthy 7 percent of Panama's GDP, on top of the billions the country nets from trade through the Panama Canal. But according to World Bank estimates, 25 percent of Panamanians lack basic sanitation and 11 percent suffer from malnutrition. The country's Indigenous people, representing almost 13 percent of the population, have been almost completely shut out of any benefits Panama has reaped from the offshore business; most still lack access to clean water and health care.

As Roberto Eisenmann, founder of Panama City's daily newspaper *La Prensa*, put it, "We still have two countries—a First World country that's going gangbusters, and half an hour away, a Fourth World country." Virtually all the elites benefiting from Panama's offshore industry are foreigners, including both its clientele and its main service providers: skilled workers from abroad. Locals have quite a different experience. Panama City ranks number eight on the list of the ten most violent cities in the world by per capita murder rate. The country is regularly rocked by protests against inequality, poverty, and corruption. While Panama has no army, its border-defense officers are often deployed to quell these social movements. For all its wealth, Panama remains stunted by inequality, violence, and a weak democracy that occasionally verges into authoritarian rule.

But the finance curse doesn't just happen in former colonies. What happens offshore never really stays offshore. Increasingly often, the curse washes up on the doorsteps of the world's wealthiest metropolitan financial centers.

The United Kingdom itself, long considered the beating heart of offshore finance, is now "home to some of Europe's poorest areas," with a full one-fifth of the population living in poverty. At the same time, the country's capital has earned the nickname "Londongrad" because of the vast wealth it has attracted from the former Soviet Empire—wealth on a scale that has distorted the British legal system, its press freedoms, and even its housing supply. Former British home secretary Priti Patel acknowledged this in a 2022 speech to Parliament about the outsized economic and political influence Russian oligarchs attained in the country. "Putin's cronies," she said, "have hidden dirty money in the U.K. and . . . abuse the U.K.'s open society." Shortly afterward, a Conservative member of Parliament rose to read aloud a list of U.K. lawyers employed by the oligarchs to intimidate British journalists into suppressing negative stories about the capture of the country's institutions by wealthy foreign elites.

Evidence of the finance curse is abundantly visible and keenly felt by locals. So much so that journalist Oliver Bullough, who writes frequently on offshore finance, has developed a sideline business in "kleptocracy tours": he simply drives tourists around London to show them where the ultra-rich—not only from Russia but also from Nigeria, Kazakhstan, Libya, and the Arab Peninsula—have bought up the stately mansions once occupied by the British nobility. The houses are rarely occupied, since they are purchased not as residences but mainly as investments in which to park looted and laundered money. As several of the U.K.-based wealth managers I interviewed explained, their clients don't mind spending tens of millions of pounds on homes they rarely—if ever—visit. For the buyers, the homes are a safer bet to hold their value than cash deposited in corrupt banks back home.

Meanwhile, local people who actually work in London and need places to live are increasingly priced out of the city's housing market. This problem extends across all of the United Kingdom's urban areas, where housing purchases by buyers registered in foreign countries—mostly tax havens—doubled between 2011 and 2021. This has driven up residential real estate prices by nearly 20 percent, forcing many locals to spend half their paychecks just to keep a roof over their heads. At the same time, they're receiving fewer and poorer-quality public services, because the use of offshore shell companies to purchase real estate allows foreign buyers to avoid millions of dollars in sales taxes for each property, depriving the U.K. government of much-needed revenue.

The increasing displacement and immiseration of the United Kingdom's local population by wealthy people from abroad are part and parcel of the "boomerang" effect of colonialism that Aimé Césaire first noted in 1950. The country that originated the common law and made it the operating system for its global empire now finds these and other tools of imperial power turned against it on its home turf. Not only did the United Kingdom's ancient democracy come under siege by oligarchs flush with offshore wealth but—as noted by legal scholar Kojo Koram—the native population ended up worse off, since the "dismantling of Britain's welfare state was intimately related to global systems of tax avoidance." For example, while one part of the British government turned a blind eye to Goldman Sachs using offshore accounts to dodge more than $48 million in U.K. taxes, another arm of the state was simultaneously closing libraries, youth centers, and other vital social services in the name of austerity.

A similar paradox of plenty afflicts Luxembourg, the corporate tax haven of choice for more than 120 banks and $3.5 trillion worth of mutual fund shares. Thanks to its robust financial services sector, which contributes 31 percent of the country's economic production and employs 12 percent of its population, the grand duchy boasts the highest per capita GDP on the European continent, far outstripping its nearest rivals: Ireland, Norway, and Switzerland. At first blush, Luxembourg would appear to be in terrific shape—a wealthy democracy thriving in the center of Western Europe.

However, according to economist Gabriel Zucman, Luxembourg's role as a leading tax haven has benefited foreigners at the expense of locals. Almost 60 percent of the country's workforce is composed of foreign workers—most of whom don't live in Luxembourg but commute in from neighboring countries. Through their high salaries and benefits packages, these individuals reap a huge share of the country's wealth: as Zucman found, a full one-third of Luxembourg's GDP goes into the pockets of foreigners. "The situation," Zucman writes, "is unique in the world and in history: no independent nation, no matter how small and open to international trade, has ever paid such a share of its income abroad." As a result, Luxembourg's society is fracturing along expats-versus-locals lines, both in economic and political terms.

As Zucman documents, inequality in the grand duchy has skyrocketed over the past decades, with poverty doubling since 1980, while real wages for ordinary Luxembourgers stagnated for more than twenty years. Salaries for expat wealth managers have exploded, tripling housing prices in Luxembourg City, but this new wealth has not benefited the local economy. Thanks to Luxembourg's tax policies, public institutions such as the educational system are in "accelerated decline." The result, Zucman argues, is that Luxembourg has become less a country than a free-trade zone for the international ultra-rich.

This pattern casts an ominous shadow across all of Europe's democracies. Luxembourg's full membership in the European Union is based on the premise that its government represents the citizens of the duchy. But having "sold its sovereignty" to multinational corporations, Luxembourg has made itself the political arm of international finance, effectively giving those multinationals voting and veto privileges over European public policy.

Whatever benefits the tax-haven business might bring to a country, it seems to be a Faustian bargain. Some countries may rack up impressive economic growth, but as the cases of Panama and Luxembourg—as well as Jersey and the BVI—illustrate, the wealth they create generally goes to corrupt politicians or to expat workers in the financial services industry. These gains don't just bypass local people but are often made at their expense, in the form of rising prices for housing, food, and other necessities. Locals are also hit hard by regressive taxes on payrolls and consumption, imposed to make up for losses from low or nil taxes on income and investments. As for politics, the rights of local people are often curtailed, lest they interfere with the preferences of transnational capital and its agents. Inquiry and transparency are discouraged amid threats of detention and deportation.

Just a month after the Panama Papers broke, more than three hundred of the world's leading economists—among them Thomas Piketty, Nobel Prize winner Angus Deaton, and Olivier Blanchard, former chief economist for the International Monetary Fund—released an open letter calling for an end to tax havens, or at least to the financial secrecy they provide. "There is no economic justification for them to continue," they declared. World leaders are unlikely to heed their advice. For one thing, as all the offshore leaks have shown, many of the people empowered to change the laws are themselves deeply enmeshed in the world of offshore finance. This includes not only the leaders of wealthy countries but also those of more economically precarious nations that have become dependent on the foreign currency and transaction fees that offshore finance brings them. It is extremely difficult to disentangle a country from the tax-haven business once that industry becomes a monoculture, dominating the local economy as well as the government. There is often nothing left to build on once the offshore business dries up or leaves.

A better solution might be to offer an alternative development model, based on that of countries that escaped the resource curse. Norway, which is endowed with vast oil resources, used its long tradition of strong, trustworthy democratic institutions to distribute the country's burgeoning wealth in a relatively equitable fashion. But what of countries already plagued by poverty or struggling to establish good governance after colonial rule?

Botswana is frequently mentioned as a success story in this context. The small nation, a British protectorate until 1966, used to be among the very poorest globally. But since the discovery of rich mineral resources—mostly diamonds, but also copper, nickel, and coal—it has quickly become an upper-middle-income country, while at the same time boasting one of the least-corrupt governments in the world. Among the keys to Botswana's success has been economic diversification: the refusal to put all its eggs in one basket. This enables the country to maintain its independence, not only fiscally but politically.

It is unclear how applicable this model is to nations considering the move to offshore finance or already entangled with it. The lesson from Botswana is that sources of new wealth must be managed in the public interest, to ensure that their influence on the economy and society truly benefits the country, not just local elites and international investors. But is that really possible when a source of wealth is not owned and controlled by the nation—as Botswana's diamonds are—and is highly mobile, as mineral reserves are not?

Unlike natural resources, the wealth involved in offshore finance doesn't originate within a single nation's boundaries. Elites can easily move their fortunes to other countries should an economic or political situation cease to suit their interests. This gives them the power to dictate terms to host countries. Maybe the economist Jeffrey Sachs, one of the hundreds of signatories to the letter stating that tax havens have "no economic justification," was correct in his simple conclusion: "They just need to end."

CHAPTER 5

This Side of Fiscal Paradise

I N *THE GREAT GATSBY*, NARRATOR Nick Carraway tries to learn the hidden ways of wealth by buying a set of books that promise "to unfold the shining secrets that only Midas and Morgan and Mæcenas knew." His tragedy is that he ends up learning about wealth and secrets the hard way: by entering the social milieu of the rich, and only then finding out how destructive, deceptive, and even criminal their world can be. Although my journey went in the opposite direction—first growing up among the rich, then reading books about them—I reached a similar end point as Carraway's. But instead of telling you about careless people who smash things up, I've tried to show how careful and clever people have built a destructive global system that affects all of us.

That's why this book tells the story of that system, rather than recounting the lifestyles of the rich and famous. As C. Wright Mills noted, the problem with plutocrats isn't personal—it's systemic. That is, "power is not of a man. Wealth does not center in the person of the wealthy. . . . To be wealthy, to have power requires access to major institutions." Thus, when the late Queen Elizabeth II turned up in the Paradise Papers, and when elected heads of state who ran on anti-corruption platforms were exposed in the Pandora Papers as money launderers and tax cheats, the important part of those stories was not their personalities but the system that made possible their selective exemption from their own countries' rule of law. Offshore finance is the institution that positioned them in a shared space of opposition to democracy, capitalism, and even—thanks to offshore's connection with lucrative projects that destroy the earth's environment—civilizational survival.

Offshore finance doesn't just make a few people exceptionally wealthy and powerful: it diminishes other citizens' ability to participate in the political system on equal terms, and it weakens the institutions meant to serve the common good. It seizes state power that is "of the people, by the people, for the people" and transforms it into an instrument serving a profoundly anti-democratic agenda. The impacts are felt worldwide—for example, when organizations like the OECD or the E.U. Parliament fail to constrain legal and financial abuses occurring in tax havens. The contrast between the radical freedom for elites and the repression of ordinary citizens is most keenly felt in the offshore financial centers themselves.

For those outside the ranks of the ultra-rich, all of this seems like a huge and dangerous step backward into financialized quasi-feudalism. To understand why the plutocrats benefiting from the offshore system might see things differently, it is helpful to recall that they do not rely on many of the public institutions the rest of us need. They rarely educate their children in the public schools, don't depend on national health-care systems, and don't require a state pension in order to retire. If all those institutions—created and maintained through representative democracy and the tax contributions of generations—disappeared tomorrow, the elite would be fine, at least in the short and medium term. In fact, they would be better off, because they could keep for themselves the relatively small share of their wealth they now pay via their taxes to support those institutions.

And if the nation becomes a crumbling ruin, with cratering levels of health and education outcomes, or roads and bridges falling to pieces, then what of it? Offshore wealth shields plutocrats from most of these ill effects almost indefinitely. In the short term, they may adapt to local anarchy as the ultra-rich of Brazil and Mexico have done, using helicopters to commute a few blocks to work or to ferry their children to school, high above the crime-ridden streets where their fellow citizens must struggle to survive as best they can. In the long term, when their adaptations cease to protect them, they can retreat to luxury underground bunkers—complete with bowling alleys!—or even to outer space. The ultimate display of wealth and power is to escape not only the laws of the state but also the laws of gravity. For now, content to slip the surly bonds of society, they place the burdens of taxes and legal accountability on the shoulders of the rest of us.

To some, the perspective of these elite clients of offshore finance might seem shortsighted, even irrational. But as the late French sociologist Bruno Latour wrote, they are making a rational calculation: they believe, he argued, that the wealth they accumulate by undermining the rule of law, weakening democracy, and gaming the economic system will purchase their escape from a collapsing society and environment. They need only to fill their coffers now by maximizing the benefits they extract from lawlessness and environmental destruction. This project of freedom for a tiny "elect" at the expense of the rest can only advance when secrecy provides protection from scrutiny.

Social theorist Douglas Rushkoff, who was invited to advise these plutocrats on their escape plans (at a secret location, of course), called their strategy "the insulation equation." Fueled by nearly limitless money and power, the billionaires were uninterested in and rather bemused by Rushkoff's attempts to engage them in considering human solidarity and collective action to save life on Earth. Instead, they wanted to know whether it was better to put shock collars on their bodyguards, to prevent them from seizing the billionaires' food supplies, or to use robot guards instead. Doomsday and mass death were problems to be escaped, not solved.

On a day-to-day basis, what happens in offshore financial centers may appear to be merely a matter of bureaucratic paper pushing and money moving: antiseptic and bloodless. As one of the offshore wealth managers I interviewed put it, "Most of what we do is paperwork." But the impact of those papers, words, numbers, and rules is very material. They create systems of enduring economic and political inequality. Sometimes, these conditions are so extreme that they produce unnecessary suffering and even death, such as when tax cuts for the ultra-rich mean steep cuts to essential public services providing food, housing, medical care, education, and transportation. This happens not only in the poorer and more peripheral states in the offshore system but, increasingly often, in the wealthiest and most established financial centers of the world.

A growing body of research shows that even in rich countries, austerity programs that cut those basic necessities dramatically increase death rates via mechanisms such as infant mortality and adult suicide. Friedrich Engels, a sometime writing partner of Karl Marx, coined the phrase *sozialer Mord*, or "social murder," to describe such phenomena, in which the design and functioning of the social order contributes to needless suffering and untimely deaths. Engels, who was the heir to a textile factory fortune in England, had witnessed the ravages of the industrial system himself. That it operated as a disembodied, invisible hand in workers' lives made it all the more insidious. Social murder, he wrote, is "disguised," and "none can defend himself . . . because no one sees the murderer." He identified the same problem that offshore finance now presents to the world: How do you fight a system that is both dangerous and faceless?

Colonialism was very different in this respect: it did most of its "dirty work" in the open, spearheaded by identifiable individuals and organizations. The exploitation and death created by that system were witnessed by many, including the artists and historians who documented it in real time. There was nothing hidden about it—and that led to decades of violent uprisings and rebellions. We don't see that with offshore finance. The skillful deployment of secrecy and complexity neatly solved the biggest problem colonialism ever faced: the revolt of the colonized. Without awareness of exploitation, without an identifiable source of domination, there can be no resistance.

But many people, even in what used to be considered stable, developed Western democracies, sense that something is really wrong. They vote, but their political leaders seem to ignore them; they pay their taxes, but their hospitals and schools are being closed, or the quality of services is plummeting. They work hard, but their social, political, and economic systems don't seem to work for them. In this sense, the offshore financial system is Colonialism 2.0, with much of the exploitation and injustice of the original version, updated with a postmodern twist: the colonizers are no longer the agents of individual nations but instead represent borderless capital, and the colonies they exploit include much of the "free" world. Worse yet, the vast majority of the colonized have no idea that they are being preyed upon by an offshore elite that has largely liberated itself from the concept of nationality, except as a convenience to protect their property rights.

Unlike the original version, Colonialism 2.0 is "de-territorialized," meaning that power is exerted by actors—both individuals and organizations—who aren't tied down or locatable in any particular place. The same can be said of their wealth. The organizations, mostly companies, are multinational. The individual elites obtain and abandon citizenship as it suits them. For both groups, their assets move more or less frictionlessly to whichever locale offers the best opportunity to grow without constraints, such as taxes and regulations.

The original subjects of colonialism could locate the people exploiting them, and even see them face-to-face. That isn't possible now. Demagogues and fascists thrive in such conditions, because no one needs to be convinced that society is falling apart: they just want to be told whose fault it is. So instead of colonial revolts, we get populism and pogroms. This is where offshore intersects with the global rise of anti-democratic authoritarian movements, as economist Thomas Piketty and historian Ruth Ben-Ghiat have pointed out. Even in a world beset by conspiracy theories, it's remarkably difficult to convey how much of what's wrong with democracy and capitalism is due to the distortion of those systems by private capital flowing around the world in secret. It is much easier to convince people that the problem lies with individuals they can see: perhaps immigrants or those who worship differently. One of the most important tasks for modern sociology is to counteract this simmering "war of all against all" by exposing some of the systemic sources of these conflicts.

What then must we do? This famous question was posed by Russian novelist Leo Tolstoy in his well-known 1886 book-length essay on wealth, poverty, and exploitation in a feudal agrarian society. He followed it in 1900 with another essay posing an even better question: "Need it be so?" Tolstoy, who was a hereditary landowner himself and had inherited more than six hundred serfs—quasi-enslaved peasants attached to specific plots of land—concluded that most people simply live their lives without considering these questions, thereby perpetuating great injustices. The sociological imagination seeks to revive these neglected lines of questioning.

Responding to the challenges presented by the offshore financial system is difficult not just because of its secrecy but because of its scope. The sheer breadth of offshore's impact—social, political, economic, and even environmental—can seem overwhelming. Even transnational organizations have difficulty addressing it all. What's needed is not just a sociological imagination but a global imagination.

This is what I've been trying to build, particularly by calling attention to the transnational professionals who create and manage the offshore financial system. While the Panama, Paradise, and Pandora Papers didn't bring down that system, as some expected, they did do one great service: they put into the public domain a vast trove of data needed to show quantitatively the real costs of offshore. They gave us a good look at what used to be completely invisible.

These data also made it possible to test ideas generated by my earlier qualitative research, recounted in *Capital Without Borders*. The most important of those ideas was that wealth managers are the linchpins of the offshore financial system and that they—instead of or in addition to their clients—should be the focal points of any efforts to curtail offshore activity. Others have suspected as much, but have lacked the kind of evidence needed to make policy changes. Back in 1992, a Conservative MP named David Shaw tried to pass legislation that would have prevented U.K. lawyers and accountants from working in tax havens. Decades before his peers in government, Shaw perceived that these forms of professional expertise were being used in the former colonies to create whole economic systems based on fraud—including, but not limited to, tax evasion. Unfortunately, his bill died in the House of Commons after only one reading, never to be revived.

A few years later in Israel, legislators had a similar light-bulb moment about the importance of wealth managers, and were actually able to implement a policy initiative based on that insight. Lacking the regulatory personnel necessary to track down all of the country's tax evaders, Israeli legislators instead engaged the wealth managers in the effort to close loopholes. The legislators offered the experts the chance to play an important and positive public role in designing new legislation that would shut off many avenues for legal tax avoidance, while allowing a few to remain open—giving the professionals some financial rewards for ensuring their clients' tax compliance. This collaboration significantly reduced the flow of wealth leaving Israel, enabling the country to retain much more domestic tax revenue and investment.

For research purposes, the Israeli case was a promising development, but not enough to put my hypotheses to the test. Israel is just one country, and the policy had no direct links to any offshore financial centers. So it wasn't clear whether a strategy of focusing public policy on wealth managers could be generalized. It was only when big data on offshore finance became available following the leaks of 2016 through 2021 that it was possible to put these ideas to a rigorous global test. With a research team composed of my network scientist and mathematician colleagues at Dartmouth—Herbert Chang, Dan Rockmore, and Feng Fu—I analyzed quantitatively the pattern that my qualitative work implied: that wealth managers are at the center of interlocking networks linking elite clients to their offshore wealth and to one another.

A decade after publishing my initial claims that wealth managers are the key to the whole offshore system, this study showed mathematically that it was true. We demonstrated that when the wealth managers' network ties were disrupted—as they would be through policies targeting their activities—the whole system collapsed and oligarchs were cut off from their assets. These findings suggested that the professional intermediaries are pivotal not only in maintaining the offshore financial network but in facilitating some of its most harmful outcomes, such as exploding wealth inequality and elite corruption.

We also found support for another prediction from my qualitative research: that many oligarchs place all their offshore finances in the hands of the same small group of trusted wealth managers. This means that just a few highly connected professionals hold places of exceptional strategic importance in the offshore financial services world. Sharing the secrets of their fortunes with only a handful of experts makes sense from the plutocrats' perspective, particularly for those from more autocratic countries—such as Russia and China— where personal financial information in the wrong hands could trigger political reprisals against them and their families. Such elites tightly restrict their circle of advisers, doling out information only on a "need to know" basis and exclusively to wealth managers chosen by word of mouth from trusted family and friends. The fewer people with access to secrets, the easier it is to preserve discretion. The same principle obtains within the Mafia.

From the perspective of policymakers, this creates a very useful vulnerability that can be exploited strategically: those wealth managers represent points of "superfragility," as network scientists call it, in an offshore financial system that has otherwise been very successful at repelling intervention from outsiders. This insight can put a stop to the costly and ineffective strategies the United States, the European Union, the United Kingdom, and the OECD—among others—have deployed to combat offshore abuses and to impose sanctions. The mainstream approach, which involves chasing down the assets of wealthy individuals and multinational corporations, hasn't worked. Their assets are too mobile, and it's too easy to conceal ownership through common offshore finance techniques like the use of nominee directors or special-purpose trusts. Exerting pressure on wealth managers is much more efficient and effective, whether that pressure takes the form of rewards for cooperation with regulatory authorities (as in the Israeli case) or restrictions on the transfer of their knowledge to criminal clients.

These findings are particularly timely in relation to the Russian oligarchs sanctioned for supporting President Vladimir Putin's 2022 invasion of Ukraine. At least twenty of them are suing to have those sanctions lifted, and many more have moved key assets—including their jets, superyachts, and stock portfolios—to legal "safe havens" like Dubai, outside the reach of sanctions regimes. My work suggests that instead of or in addition to pursuing these oligarchs' wealth, policymakers could achieve their aims more effectively by forbidding wealth managers in their jurisdictions from working with sanctioned individuals. Doing so would sever many oligarchs' offshore networks in one fell swoop, cutting off key access points to their fortunes. Disrupting the expertise pipeline linking clients to offshore finance achieves the intended effects of sanctions much more directly and conclusively than seizing a particular yacht or private jet.

Once the connection to the experts has been disrupted, oligarchs cannot easily recover by obtaining new wealth managers. Many of the ultra-wealthy harbor politically sensitive, potentially explosive secrets of a financial, legal, and personal nature. As one Swiss wealth manager I interviewed put it, clients must metaphorically "undress in front of you," because all their most private information affects their fortunes and the legal-financial strategies needed to protect them. Finding wealth managers who can be trusted with such information is a lengthy and fraught process. Another wealth manager I interviewed recounted, "One of my clients said to me after years working with him, 'You know I can't sack you now. You know where everything is, you know everything about me.'"

For oligarchs cut off from their wealth managers by the sanctions strategy I'm suggesting, transferring secrets to new experts would create a substantial risk of exposure. The more people who know how the oligarchs obtained their wealth, how much they have, and where it's located, the more vulnerable they are to asset seizures and physical danger—not only from repressive governments but from opportunistic freelance criminals, who might find the oligarchs and their families ripe targets for kidnapping or extortion. In the world of offshore finance, trust is not a commodity and cannot be purchased easily from another provider.

Forbidding wealth managers from working with sanctioned clients is not a new idea; nor would it destroy the professionals' livelihoods. The policy tradition of limiting experts' provision of knowledge in the national interest stems from a set of practices developed during the Cold War to restrict the transfer of know-how linked to nuclear, chemical, and biological weapons. These strategies have a promising record of success as a nonmilitary route to addressing international conflicts. For example, Iran's decision to enter into the 2015 agreement that limited its nuclear program was credited in part to a policy of restricting the ruling regime's access to legal-financial experts, so that the country's leadership "could not access its foreign exchange assets held abroad," according to a Congressional Research Service report. The prospect that cooperation with U.S. demands could restore links to those experts, and to the $100 to $150 billion of Iranian assets they managed in overseas accounts, eventually brought Iran's leaders back to the negotiating table.

That such rules are now being applied by the United States, European Union, and others to the financial, legal, and accounting expertise of wealth managers indicates growing recognition that offshore finance can threaten national and international security. Switzerland has already prosecuted some wealth managers who serve sanctioned oligarchs. Recently, a court in Geneva handed down criminal convictions and a large fine to four wealth managers who allowed a sanctioned Russian national known as "Putin's wallet" to deposit millions in Zurich bank accounts; the funds were suspected to be part of Putin's personal fortune. The United States has also banned the provision to sanctioned individuals of certain forms of offshore expertise, including accountancy and corporate formation services, which are crucial for creating and maintaining the structures that shroud oligarchs' assets in secrecy. The European Union and the United Kingdom have implemented similar measures, banning international law and tax experts based in those jurisdictions from serving sanctioned Russian oligarchs. The bans are backed by penalties including huge fines and imprisonment. The highly tailored nature of this strategy, targeting only the expertise linking sanctioned individuals to their offshore wealth, makes it far less morally fraught than broad-based sanctions, which can deprive whole nations of vital resources like grain, medical supplies, and fuel. Meanwhile, the wealth managers remain free to carry on business as usual and maintain their livelihoods, provided they stop working with sanctioned clients.

All of this sets a promising precedent for the future, in terms of combatting offshore abuses. So does the extraordinary solidarity shown by many of the world's leading offshore financial centers following the invasion of Ukraine. The war quickly galvanized a coalition of nations that usually compete to attract Russian oligarchs' fortunes. Instead, perhaps for the first time, the United States, Switzerland, Britain, Monaco, and the European Union cooperated in freezing, seizing, and expelling the wealth belonging to Putin's allies. Even Cyprus—so dependent on Putin's cronies that it has been described as a "Russian bank with dirty money posing as an E.U. state"—risked the wrath of its top clients by breaking off an agreement to let Russian planes use Cypriot airspace and Russian naval ships dock in Cypriot ports. Singapore stopped short of individual sanctions, but the popular tax haven made the "almost unprecedented" move to shut out Russian banks.

These were remarkable developments in their own right, quite apart from their impact on the war, because they showed that offshore centers *could* act collectively in the best interests of society by refusing to aid and abet kleptocrats. For decades, offshore centers—ranging from giants like the United States and Switzerland to the small palm-fringed "fiscal paradises" of Nevis and Vanuatu—have insisted that this could not be done under any circumstances. But now they have demonstrated that they are willing and able, when they wish, to break down their own walls of silence and complicity, even though this threatens their core business model.

This represents one possible future for the offshore world, in which it rights its own wrongs. It remains to be seen whether this crisis-driven cooperation can be sustained. Another possible trajectory is more common historically: many systems that create extreme imbalances of power and wealth simply self-destruct.

The Roman historian Pliny offers an instructive case study of this dynamic. Almost two thousand years ago, he wrote of a system that concentrated wealth and power so effectively that it destroyed the Roman Republic. The system was called the *latifundia*, and it worked like this: each wealthy Roman who acquired at least six hundred acres of land automatically received a seat in the Senate. From there, they could influence every area of public life, from taxation to the military and foreign policy. Unsurprisingly, those wealthy landowners used their political authority to favor their own economic interests at the expense of their fellow citizens. Among other privileges, they exempted themselves from land taxes, which allowed their wealth to increase at an accelerated rate. The rapid growth of their combined economic and political power profoundly changed society. Most importantly, their development of large scale for-profit farms required armies of landless peasants, as well as slaves, to generate maximum revenue. As the *latifundistas*—the absentee landlords in the Senate— acquired increasingly large tracts of land, they turned many of Italy's formerly independent small farmers into employees, working the land for a share of the masters' harvests. Widespread poverty ensued.

This economic destabilization of ordinary citizens alarmed Pliny, since it triggered a reversal in Rome's centuries-long advance toward a broadly representative democracy, in which commoners could wield power alongside the nobility. As he saw it, hungry, desperate people were no longer free. Hence his stark conclusion that a system producing immense wealth and power for a few would destroy the very society that gave rise to it. *Latifundia perdidere Italiam,* he wrote: "The latifundia have been the ruin of Italy."

The latifundia was so successful in making a small group of nobles ever more wealthy and powerful that it spread to Rome's territories in Africa, becoming the model from which the Roman Empire and the colonial plantation later arose. Through this lineage, the institution that so troubled Pliny is the ancient ancestor of the contemporary system of offshore finance.

The family resemblance is clear: the offshore financial system is just a new way of concentrating wealth and power into too few hands, undermining both democracy and collective economic prosperity. The resemblance extends even to the finance curse, since Pliny's contemporaries noted that the latifundia's extreme inequalities gave rise to pervasive corruption and moral decay. In the corrupt leaders whose names and faces appeared in media coverage of the Panama, Paradise, and Pandora Papers, we find modern incarnations of the rentier senators of Rome. Can we prevent them from bringing down the political order again?

Some put their hopes on prosecution following the big offshore leaks of 2016 through 2021, but that hasn't panned out. As Mossack Fonseca told the world in a terse public statement (just over one thousand words) following the release of the Panama Papers: if you don't like what we do, change the laws, because we didn't break any. While that claim turned out to be somewhat exaggerated—both Mossack and Fonseca spent a few months in jail—the subsequent rarity of prosecutions stemming from the offshore leaks was striking, as was the even smaller number of convictions. Whatever one may think of them morally, many uses of offshore are legal; the rest are often so complex that no one can prove that they're illegal.

By my count, there have been fewer than two dozen convictions worldwide based on the tens of millions of records made public via offshore leaks in the eight years since the Panama Papers broke. These cases are difficult to make, so with enough time, there may be more in future. But the clients of the offshore financial system tend to have the best lawyers and the deepest pockets, so they can dig in for long fights that even wealthy countries' governments can't afford to pursue. Even those few people convicted as a result of information exposed in the offshore leaks have largely escaped punishment, thanks to their wealth and power.

For example, in the summer of 2016, soccer star Lionel Messi was convicted of tax fraud by a court in Spain, in part because of data revealed in the Panama Papers; but he never spent any time behind bars for the crime, having paid a fine in lieu of serving his twenty-one-month sentence. In 2018, former Pakistani prime minister Nawaz Sharif was sentenced to fourteen years in prison for corruption revealed by the Panama Papers; but a few months after his conviction, he got permission to travel to London for "medical treatment" and simply stayed there, living in one of his family's luxury homes for the next four years. In 2023, he persuaded a court in the capital of Islamabad to let him return to Pakistan without being arrested, so that he could once again run for political office.

So for these and many other reasons reviewed in this book, I'm not optimistic about the legal route for stemming abuses of the offshore financial system. Legal change is necessary, but experience shows that it won't suffice as the sole or primary response to the offshore crisis. Rather, I put my hope in changing social norms. Attitudes about right and wrong shift much more quickly than laws, and at the end of the day, rich people still care about what the rest of us think of them. This has been one of the biggest surprises of my work on offshore finance: the people you'd expect to be laughing all the way to the bank are as sensitive as anyone else to the power of shame. This also goes for wealth managers, the architects of the offshore system. It sounds crazy, but this theme came up again and again in my own research: social stigma is kryptonite for offshore elites. "I'm very good at my job, and I should be able to hold my head high," said one wealth manager I interviewed, "so I resent the tax shaming and tsk-tsking at offshore these days." Even the monthly magazine for wealth managers has bemoaned how the once-respectable profession has come to be "regarded with disdain and stigmatized."

The power of shame and stigma is such that when the U.K. tax authorities conducted a study on deterrents to elite tax evasion, it found that the threat to publish evaders' names in the newspaper was far more effective than fines or lawsuits. This fear of socio-emotional consequences is also why oligarchs have gone to such extraordinary lengths worldwide to harass and silence journalists, politicians, and other investigators who might expose them to condemnation. This was illustrated vividly in the weeks after the 2022 invasion of Ukraine, when Putin—who had made no public response to the crushing economic sanctions imposed on his country—went on television to complain about "cancel culture," because European orchestras were refusing to play Tchaikovsky. Soon afterward, when the European Union threatened to deny tourist visas to Russian elites, billionaire Moscow-media figure Vladimir Solovyov suggested that Putin should nuke Europe to retaliate for the perceived humiliation.

Not only do status punishments work on these elites, they work more quickly and effectively than many laws do. While the ultra-rich can easily repel formal punishments such as lawsuits, threats to their reputations and their social status are more difficult to combat and provoke their strongest responses.

So I'll close this book with the same advice I give to the tax agencies and multinational organizations that seek my advice on how to stop abuses of the offshore financial system: use social forces to your advantage. Law changes slowly, as it should. But public sentiment can be shifted more rapidly and with great effect. Stigmatization, in particular, is a weapon of immense but often misdirected power. Too rarely is it turned on genuinely bad actors, but when it is, stigma can move the otherwise immovable. In the early 2000s, it swiftly transformed corporate practices that had been complete non-issues previously: legal practices like tax avoidance and the use of sweatshop labor became toxic to brand reputation.

Could public sentiment shift to stigmatize the use of offshore finance? If there's any chance of that, the first step is creating awareness of the problem: that's one reason I wrote this book. The second step is organizing displays of disapproval. Other people specialize in that, such as social movement leaders and the new cadre of social media influencers. In recent years, we've seen the former bring the long-dormant U.S. labor movement roaring back to life, while the latter convinced thousands of young people to eat laundry detergent pods for likes. By comparison, galvanizing a grassroots movement to condemn the use of offshore finance should be a breeze. In a battle of stigmatization versus structures of exploitation, of grassroots social movements versus global finance, bet on the social forces to prevail.

ACKNOWLEDGMENTS

I'M FORTUNATE TO HAVE such a patient and supportive family, who let me disappear into writing and revising this book for months at a time; I missed a lot of board games and dinners, and will enjoy making it up to them! Special thanks go to my mother, for taking adolescent me on her business trip to Peru long ago. The sights at Cusco, among others, provided insights that proved important for this book.

My high-school history teacher, Steve Sommers, also contributed to this book with his unforgettably enlightening course on imperialism. At university, I was lucky enough to take a few classes with Terry Karl, around the time she was doing research on the paradox of plenty. Both lit a fire of curiosity about colonialism and political economy that fueled the creation of this book.

The editorial team led by Alane Mason, with help from Sasha Levitt and Caroline Adams, midwifed this manuscript so that it could reach a general readership. I'm very grateful to them, as well as to the editing magic of Arthur Goldwag. Finally, everyone should be so lucky as to have an agent like Jim Levine: an invaluable source of wisdom and industry experience.

Work on this book was funded in part by a Public Scholars award from the National Endowment for the Humanities (#FZ-292684-23). My research was also supported by internal funding from the Dean of the Faculty, the Ethics Center, and the Rockefeller Center for Public Policy at Dartmouth College. For the history recounted in chapter 3, I'm grateful for the assistance of the staff at the Bahamas National Archives, particularly that of Ms. Tomoko Smith.

NOTES

INTRODUCTION

5 **Even those who *do* specialize:** The term was used in congressional testimony by Senator Carl Levin (D-MI) in a statement before the U.S. Permanent Subcommittee on Investigations on November 18, 2003: "The US Tax Shelter Industry: The Role of Accountants, Lawyers, and Financial Professionals."

8 **I could invest this time:** See example job listings in my article "Trust and Estate Planning: A Profession and Its Contribution to Socio-Economic Inequality," *Sociological Forum* 27 (2012): 825–46.

10 **In consequence, he wrote:** From the 1950 English compilation of Georg Simmel's work translated into English: *The Sociology of Georg Simmel*, trans. and ed. Kurt H. Wolff (New York: Free Press, 1950), 404.

10 **Fieldwork, as Van Maanen:** John Van Maanen, *Tales of the Field: On Writing Ethnography* (Chicago: University of Chicago Press, 1988), 83.

12 **Others were conscience-stricken:** A topic I've written about at length elsewhere, particularly in "Turning Vice into Virtue: Institutional Work and Professional Misconduct," *Human Relations*, 72 (2018): 1464–96.

CHAPTER 1: THE UNAUTHORIZED BIOGRAPHY OF A
SECRETIVE SYSTEM

15 **Occasional reminders crop up:** This was the case of the late Robert Brockman. Michael Levenson, "U.S. Brings 'Largest Ever Tax Charge' Against Tech Executive," *New York Times*, October 15, 2020.

16 **Like gold and jewels:** Georg Simmel, *The Sociology of Georg Simmel*, trans. and ed. Kurt H. Wolff (Glencoe, IL: Free Press, 1950), 342–43.

17 **Move your fortune to:** Anne Michel, Emily Menkes, and Kimberley Porteous, "Secret Files Reveal Rothschild's Offshore Domain," International Consortium of Investigative Journalists, April 11, 2013.

17 **These include infomercial king:** See Aaron Gell, "'That's Not All!': Kevin Trudeau, the World's Greatest Salesman, Makes One Last Pitch," *Business Insider*, January 20, 2015.

17 **Since 2011, Trudeau has:** See this 2009 announcement from the U.S. Federal Trade Commission: https://www.ftc.gov/news-events/news/press -releases/2009/01/judge-orders-kevin-trudeau-pay-more-37-million-false -claims-about-weight-loss-book.

17 **Consider the case of:** Rory Mulholland, "'The Most Expensive Divorce in History' Ends After Russian Billionaire Reaches Deal with Ex-wife," *Telegraph*, October 21, 2015.

17 **Although a Swiss court:** On the settlement, see Vicky Ward in *Town & Country*, "*T&C* Exclusive: Inside the World's Most Expensive Divorce," October 20, 2015.

18 **For example, the destruction of:** Victor Galaz et al., "Tax Havens and Global Environmental Degradation," *Nature Ecology and Evolution*, 2 (2018): 1352–57.

18 **The former president of Chile:** Agence France-Presse, "Chile Sinks Controversial Mining Project over Environmental Concerns," *Barron's*, January 18, 2023.

18 **According to the Financial Action Task Force:** See this 2021 Financial Action Task Force Report, "Money Laundering from Environmental Crime": https://www.fatf-gafi.org/content/dam/fatf-gafi/reports/Money -Laundering-from-Environmental-Crime.pdf.

19 **Singapore, an island city:** For the "Switzerland of Asia" quote, see Chanyaporn Chanjaroen, Cathy Chan, and David Ramli, "Financial Firms Are Flocking to Singapore but Hong Kong Keeps Its Edge," *Time*, October 6, 2023. On the research center, see this Reuters news service story of September 7, 2023: "Singapore Opens Research Centre to Fight Rising Sea Levels," https://www.reuters.com/world/asia-pacific/singapore-opens-research -centre-fight-rising-sea-levels-2023-09-07/.

19 **At the current pace of:** On the destruction of the mangrove wetlands, see Katrina Jurn, Joseph Lavallee, and Lawrence King, "Environmental Destruction in the New Economy: Offshore Finance and Mangrove Forest Clearance in Grand Cayman," *Geoforum* 97 (2018): 155–68.

19 **UC Berkeley economist Gabriel Zucman:** For the source of this estimate,

see Gabriel Zucman, *The Hidden Wealth of Nations* (Chicago: University of Chicago Press, 2015).

20   **The mammoth size of:** Ronen Palan, Richard Murphy, and Christian Chavagneux, *Tax Havens: How Globalization Really Works* (Ithaca, NY: Cornell University Press, 2010).

20   **Those of us who live:** Casey Michel, *American Kleptocracy* (New York: St. Martin's, 2021).

20   **For many high-net-worth:** Oliver Bullough, "The Great American Tax Haven: Why the Super-Rich Love South Dakota," *Guardian*, November 14, 2019.

20   **Closed commercial systems ring-fenced:** See this 2019 summary by historian Grant Kleiser, "An Empire of Free Ports": https://clements.umich.edu/an-empire-of-free-ports/.

21   **The establishment of free ports:** See this 2022 essay by Kleiser, "Free Ports in the Atlantic World": https://www.oxfordbibliographies.com/display/document/obo-9780199730414/obo-9780199730414-0357.xml.

21   **$110 billion:** Alstadsæter et al., *Global Tax Evasion Report*.

22   **More than twenty years ago:** See page 2 of the transcript of *Tax Me if You Can,* a 2004 *Frontline* documentary film: www.pbs.org/wgbh/pages/frontline/shows/tax/etc/script.html.

22   **The surcharge Rossotti estimated:** According to this 2023 working paper by Niels Johannesen et al., "The Offshore World According to FATCA: New Evidence on the Foreign Wealth of U.S. Households," https://www.irs.gov/pub/irs-soi/23rpfatcaevidenceforeignwealth.pdf.

22   **By 2018, the top 1 percent:** Emmanuel Saez and Gabriel Zucman, *The Triumph of Injustice: How the Rich Dodge Taxes and How to Make Them Pay* (New York: W. W. Norton, 2019).

22   **Other new research using:** See page 15 in this 2021 NBER Working Paper (No. 28542) using IRS audit data: "Tax Evasion at the Top of the Income Distribution: Theory and Evidence," by John Guyton, Patrick Langetieg, Daniel Reck, Max Risch, and Gabriel Zucman, http://gabriel-zucman.eu/files/GLRRZ2021.pdf.

23   **By some estimates, that's:** Estimate by Princeton sociologist Matthew Desmond, in a National Public Radio interview on March 23, 2023: https://www.npr.org/sections/health-shots/2023/03/21/1164275807/poverty-by-america-matthew-desmond-inequality.

23   **Far more is known about:** See, for example, the detailed global data available in the United Nations Office on Drugs and Crime's *World Drug Report*:

https://www.unodc.org/unodc/en/data-and-analysis/world-drug-report
-2023.html.

24 **This was driven by Jefferson's:** Thomas Jefferson, *Autobiography of Thomas Jefferson, 1743–1790* ([1821]; New York: G. P. Putnam's Sons / Knicker-bocker Press, 1914), 58.

24 **Thus, Paine advocated for:** Thomas Paine, *The Rights of Man* (London: J. S. Jordan, 1792), vol. 2.

24 **About 140 years later:** The quotation is from Representative Dan V. Stevens of Nebraska, delivered in 1913 comments on the tax bill that became the Sixteenth Amendment to the U.S. Constitution, and entered into the *Congressional Record*, Appendix, 63rd Congress, 1st Session, pp. 78–79. Almost identical language, warning of the threat of "abnormal fortunes," was used to raise the issue again on the floor of Congress in 1916 by Representative William Cox of Indiana and Representative Samuel J. Tribble of Georgia. These remarks can be found in the *Congressional Record*, vol. 53, part 11, p. 10732, and the Appendix, p. 1529, respectively.

24 **These claims about wealth's:** For a summation of this research, see Thomas Piketty, *Capital in the Twenty-First Century* (Cambridge, MA: Harvard University Press, 2014).

25 **Indeed, the true extent:** Johannesen et al., "The Offshore World According to FATCA."

25 **The true extent of wealth:** See page 8 in Pinçon-Charlot's 1998 book, *Grand Fortunes: Dynasties of Wealth in France.* (Trans. Andrea Lyn Secara.) New York: Algora Publishing.

25 **Even trusted sources, like:** Arthur B. Kennickell, "Ponds and Streams: Wealth and Income in the U.S., 1989 to 2007," Finance and Economics Discussion Series (Federal Reserve Board, Washington, DC, 2009–13).

25 **"because at high wealth levels":** Gilles Keating, Michael O'Sullivan, Anthony Shorrocks, Jim B. Davies, Rodrigo Lluberas, and Antonios Koutsoukis, *Global Wealth Report 2013* (Zurich: Credit Suisse AG, 2013), 23.

26 **For example, Americans underestimate:** Michael Norton and Dan Ariely, "Building a Better America, One Wealth Quintile at a Time," *Perspectives on Psychological Science* 6 (2011): 9–12.

26 **Max Weber, a founding:** See Max Weber's famous essay "Bureaucracy," originally published in 1922, reprinted in English in the collection *From Max Weber*, ed. Hans Gerth and C. Wright Mills (New York: Oxford University Press, 1946), 233.

27   **Simmel observed similar strategies:** See, for example, Diego Gambetta, *Codes of the Underworld* (Princeton, NJ: Princeton University Press, 2009).

27   **As Princeton University sociologist:** Matthew Desmond, *Poverty, by America*. New York: Random House, 2023), 53.

27   **Other whistleblowers have exposed:** See, for example, Fred Alford, *Whistleblowers: Broken Lives and Organizational Power* (Ithaca, NY: Cornell University Press, 2001).

27   **In the case of offshore:** On Falciani, see the May 2016 *New Yorker* article "The Bank Robber," by Patrick Radden Keefe. On Deltour, see Simon Bowers, "LuxLeaks Whistleblower Avoids Jail After Guilty Verdict," *Guardian*, June 29, 2016.

28   **If offshore finance is really:** See one such recommendation in Patrick Wintour, "Tax Havens Have No Economic Justification, Say Top Economists," *Guardian*, May 9, 2016.

29   **The British Virgin Islands (BVI):** See this publication by the government of the British Virgin Islands: https://bvi.gov.vg/content/our-economy.

29   **Another former British colony:** Pritish Behuria, "The Political Economy of a Tax Haven: The Case of Mauritius," *Review of International Political Economy* 30 (2021): 772–800.

30   **When these and a handful:** Robert Sitkoff and Max Schanzenbach, "Jurisdictional Competition for Trust Funds: An Empirical Analysis of Perpetuities and Taxes," *Yale Law Journal*, 115 (2005): 356–437.

31   **Even broadly multinational organizations:** For more on this history of failed policy initiatives to rein in abuses of the offshore financial system, see Zucman, *The Hidden Wealth of Nations*, as well as Jason Sharman, *Havens in a Storm: The Struggle for Global Tax Regulation* (Ithaca, NY: Cornell University Press, 2006).

32   **Publicly, the reason given:** For the quote from the GAO report and the data on the more than one hundred jurisdictions that signed on to the CRS, see Noam Noked, "Should the United States Adopt CRS?," *Michigan Law Review* (July 2019).

32   **Those extra administrative costs:** William Boning et al., "A Welfare Analysis of Tax Audits Across the Income Distribution," June 2023, https://cdn.policyimpacts.org/cms/Welfare_Audits_ad1284984d.pdf.

32   **In the words of one Zurich-based:** See Zurich-based attorney Peter Cotorceanu's commentary in "Hiding in Plain Sight: How Non-US Persons Can *Legally* Avoid Reporting Under Both FATCA and GATCA," *Trusts & Trustees* 21 (2015): 1050–63.

33 **In 2013, the United States:** The United States' 2013 rank in the Financial Secrecy Index can be found here: https://thefactcoalition.org/2013 -financial-secrecy-index-released-u-s-still-a-top-offender/.

CHAPTER 2: A PLATFORM FOR ELITE INSURGENCY

34 **On Instagram and Telegram:** The *Wall Street Journal* published a feature on the bounty hunter: Margot Patrick, "Jet-Set Debt Collectors Join a Lucrative Game: Hunting the Superrich," November 7, 2017. On the party circuit, see Ashley Mears, *Very Important People: Status and Beauty on the Global Party Circuit* (Princeton, NJ: Princeton University Press, 2020).

36 **Ironically, Schultz's fortune was:** For Starbucks's tax avoidance scandals: "Starbucks to Pay £20m UK Corporate Tax," *Financial Times*, December 6, 2012; European Commission, "Commission Decides Selective Tax Advantages for Fiat in Luxembourg and Starbucks in the Netherlands Are Illegal Under EU State Aid Rules," press release, October 15, 2015, and Liz Alderman, "European Inquiry Focuses on a Mysterious Starbucks Business," *New York Times*, October 21, 2015. For Schultz's compensation: Anders Melin and Jeremy Diamond, "How Howard Schultz Earned More Than Half a Billion Dollars in Nine Years," Bloomberg, January 31, 2017.

37 **He's just one of:** Edward Luce, "Beware Elon Musk's Warped Libertarianism," *Financial Times*, May 24, 2023.

37 **"It was really U.S.":** Chris Isidore, "Here's How Elon Musk's Fortune Has Benefited from Taxpayer Help," CNN Business, November 14, 2021.

37 **Yet true to form:** Bess Levin, "Elon Musk Throws a S--t Fit over the Possibility of Being Taxed His Fair Share," *Vanity Fair*, October 27, 2021.

37 **For many elites like him:** Luce, "Beware Elon Musk's Warped Libertarianism."

38 **It means that the:** I first used the dine-and-dash metaphor in an opinion piece for the *New York Times* about the disclosure of the then president's tax returns: "Trump's Tax Avoidance Is a Tax on the Rest of Us," September 30, 2020.

38 **As social scientists and historians:** See Kojo Koram, *Uncommon Wealth: Britain and the Aftermath of Empire* (London: John Murray, 2022), and Michael Craton and Gail Saunders, *Islanders in the Stream: A History of the Bahamian People*, vol. 2, *From the Ending of Slavery to the Twenty-First Century* (Athens: University of Georgia Press, 2011).

39 **Rather, it represents an:** Raymond Craib, *Adventure Capitalism: A History*

of Libertarian Exit, from the Era of Decolonization to the Digital Age (Oakland, CA: PM Press, 2022), 198.

39 **His method of wealth:** For a wonderfully readable history of piracy, see Mark Hanna, *Pirate Nests and the Rise of the British Empire, 1570–1740* (Chapel Hill: University of North Carolina Press, 2017).

40 **While dishonesty and unfairness:** Economic sociologists recognize that markets often don't work this way. For a review of the classic economic view and a sociological response, see Adam Goldstein and Charlie Eaton, "Asymmetry by Design? Identity Obfuscation, Reputational Pressure, and Consumer Predation in U.S. For-Profit Higher Education," *American Sociological Review* 86, no. 5 (2021): 896–933.

40 **Offshore finance, however, makes:** See chapter 4 of my book *Capital Without Borders: Wealth Managers and the One Percent* (Cambridge, MA: Harvard University Press, 2016).

40 **This may be why:** Thiel's op-ed was published in the *Wall Street Journal* on September 12, 2014: https://www.wsj.com/articles/peter-thiel-competition-is-for-losers-1410535536.

For more on his efforts to fund the creation of new tax havens, see Laurie Clarke, "Crypto Millionaires Are Pouring Money into Central America to Build Their Own Cities," *MIT Technology Review*, April 20, 2022. Also see Tara Loader Wilkinson, "Seasteads: Self-Isolation for the Ultra-Wealthy," *Billionaire*, June 20, 2020. Finally, in a 2019 speech to the Manhattan Institute think tank, Thiel said, "I sort of would like the US to be a tax haven. . . . It's a very urgent question to think about." Full transcript of the speech: https://manhattan.institute/event/2019-wriston-lecture-peter-thiel.

41 **As economists Anastasia:** Anastasia Nesvetailova and Ronen Palan, *Sabotage: The Hidden Nature of Finance* (Washington, DC: PublicAffairs, 2020.)

41 **Even by financial industry:** For the collapse of Bear Stearns's funds in the Cayman Islands, see: https://www.reuters.com/article/us-bearstearns-arbitration/bear-stearns-faces-new-round-of-hedge-fund-claims-idUSN0554400820071205. For the connection to the global financial crisis, see Clea Bourne and Lee Edwards, "Producing Trust, Knowledge and Expertise in Financial Markets: The Global Hedge Fund Industry 'Re-presents' Itself," *Culture and Organization* 18 (2014): 107–22. For a roundup of most of the issues in one place, see this account: https://www.dollarsandsense.org/archives/2009/0509keeler.html.

41 **MIT finance professor Andrew:** http://web.mit.edu/Alo/www/Papers/

testimony2009.pdf; see also this discussion of hedge funds' impact on the crisis from German economist Reint Gropp: https://www.frbsf.org/economic-research/publications/economic-letter/2014/april/hedge-fund-risk-measurement-spillover-economic-crisis/.

41 **The damage offshore hedge:** See this IMF paper: https://www.imf.org/external/pubs/ft/wp/2010/wp1047.pdf.

42 **Millions worldwide were driven:** James Gallagher, "Recession 'Led to 10,000 Suicides,'" BBC News, June 12, 2014.

42 **Instead, many financial institutions:** Phillip Inman, "Wall Street Bonuses Under Fire," *Guardian*, July 30, 2009.

42 **Just one top banker:** On the one banker who was jailed: Jesse Eisinger, "Why Only One Top Banker Went to Jail for the Financial Crisis," *New York Times*, April 30, 2014; for the net loss to U.S. taxpayers, see Renae Merle, "A Guide to the Financial Crisis—Ten Years Later," *Washington Post*, September 10, 2018.

42 **Only about half the:** For the Federal Reserve estimate, see Jeanna Smialek, "The Financial Crisis Cost Every American $70,000, Fed Study Says," Bloomberg, August 13, 2018.

42 **Not for the first time:** On this risk-shifting phenomenon, see Dean Curran, "Risk Mismatches and Inequalities: Oil and Gas and Elite Risk-Classes in the U.S. and Canada," *Sociologica* 15, no. 2 (2021): 57–74.

42 **The result is what:** Michael Harrington, *The Other America* (New York: Macmillan, 1962).

42 **Secrecy then enables:** See Anthony Giddens on evasion of responsibility while taking reckless risks: "Risk and Responsibility," *Modern Law Review* 62 (1999): 1–10.

43 **So while some scholars:** See, e.g., Quinn Slobodian, *Crack-Up Capitalism* (New York: Metropolitan Books, 2023).

43 **These monopolies of wealth:** See, for example, this review: https://routledgehandbooks.com/doi/10.4324/9781315142876-3.

43 **As Mills wrote in:** C. Wright Mills, *The Power Elite* (New York: Oxford University Press, 1956), 105.

43 **A century from now:** Lucas Chancel and Thomas Piketty, "Global Income Inequality, 1820–2020: The Persistence and Mutation of Extreme Inequality," *Journal of the European Economic Association* 19, no. 6 (2021): 3025–62.

44 **"The very persistent immobilization":** Max Weber, *Economy and Society* (originally published in 1922 in German; Berkeley: University of California Press, 2013), 2:1096–97.

45 **In the words of the contemporary:** See Timur Kuran, "Why the Middle East Is Economically Underdeveloped: Historical Mechanisms of Institutional Stagnation," *Journal of Economic Perspectives* 18 (2004): 71–90.

45 **In fact, the contemporary surge:** See my 2017 *Socio-Economic Review* article, "Trusts and Financialization": https://academic.oup.com/ser/article/15/1/31/2890791.

45 **For example, a former:** From Austin Mitchell, Prem Sikka, John Christensen, Philip Morris, and Steven Filling, *No Accounting for Tax Havens* (Basildon, UK: Association for Accountancy & Business Affairs, 2002).

45 **Although Jersey's top tax:** Leah McGrath Goodman, "Inside the World's Top Offshore Tax Shelter," *Newsweek*, January 16, 2014.

46   **It seemed like a win-win:** Oliver Bullough, "The Fall of Jersey: How a Tax Haven Goes Bust," *Guardian*, December 8, 2015. See also Helen Pidd, "Jersey's 'Secrecy Culture' Led to My Suspension, Says Former Police Chief," *Guardian*, June 12, 2012.

46 **But as Jersey natives like John Christensen:** Nicholas Shaxson, *Treasure Islands: Tax Havens and the Men Who Stole the World* (New York: Macmillan, 2014), 190.

47 **The island became a:** On Russia and South Africa, see Bullough, "The Fall of Jersey"; on Abacha, see the BBC News report of January 27, 2021, "Sani Abacha: The Hunt for the Billions Stolen by Nigeria's Ex-leader."

47 **There was also political:** "Looking into a Black Hole," *Jersey Evening Post*, May 13, 2015.

47 **This is by no means:** See Craib, *Adventure Capitalism*.

47 **Thus, British Ghanian legal:** Koram, *Uncommon Wealth*, 176.

47 **Increasingly, that power is:** Ryan Cooper, "Tax Cheats Fuel Right-Wing Extremism Around the World," *The Week*, October 4, 2021.

48 **These later came under:** On the offshore assets: Luke Harding, "Offshore Secrets of Brexit Backer Arron Banks Revealed in Panama Papers," *Guardian*, October 1, 2016. On the illegal foreign influence: Paul Waldie, "Fears of Russian Brexit Meddling Prompt Probe of British Businessman Arron Banks," *Globe and Mail*, November 1, 2017.

48 **Mercer created:** The existence of Mercer's $60 million offshore fund to sponsor right-wing political causes was revealed in the 2017 Paradise Papers; the fund was characterized as a "war chest" by *Guardian* journalist Jon Swaine in this article shortly after the Paradise Papers story broke: "Offshore Cash Helped Fund Steve Bannon's Attacks on Hillary Clinton," November 7, 2017. For details on Mercer's funding and the Brexit

campaign, see this 2018 interview by NPR's Terry Gross with British journalist Carole Cadwalladr, who broke the story about targeted use of Facebook data by Mercer's data analytics firm to sway both the Brexit vote and the 2016 U.S. presidential vote: "Reporter Shows the Links Between the Men Behind Brexit and the Trump Campaign," July 19, 2018.

48 **The leaks also exposed:** Umberto Bacchi, "Panama Papers: France's Le Pen Dynasty, Butlers and Gold Ingots Linked to Mossack Fonseca Leak," *International Business Times*, April 5, 2016.

48 **His daughter Marine, who:** Jon Henley, "Marine Le Pen promises Liberation from the EU with France-First Policies," *Guardian*, February 5, 2017.

48 **The campaign was found:** Andrew Rettman, "Illicit Russian Billions Pose Threat to EU Democracy," *EUobserver*, April 21, 2017.

49 **To attract the wealth:** Casey Michel, *American Kleptocracy* (New York: St. Martin's, 2021).

49 **These rules have destabilized:** For a review, please see my article in the *Guardian*: "'Aristocrats Are Anarchists': Why the Wealthy Back Trump and Brexit," February 7, 2019.

49 **Deripaska was already:** See the September 29, 2022, DOJ memo: https://www.justice.gov/opa/pr/russian-oligarch-oleg-vladimirovich-deripaska-and-associates-indicted-sanctions-evasion-and. See also the October 11, 2022, DOJ memo: https://www.justice.gov/opa/pr/uk-businessman-graham-bonham-carter-indicted-sanctions-evasion-benefitting-russian-oligarch.

49 **Of course, Russians aren't:** A good resource on these laundromats is the reporting by the Organized Crime and Corruption Reporting Project: https://www.occrp.org/en/the-proxy-platform/the-proxy-platform.

50 **The UAE, Saudi Arabia:** For details on this calculation and a cross-national analysis, see Annette Alstadsaeter, Niels Johannesen, and Gabriel Zucman, "Who Owns the Wealth in Tax Havens?," *Journal of Public Economics* 162 (2018): 89–100.

50 **In one particularly egregious:** See this detailed investigation by OCCRP: https://www.occrp.org/en/russianlaundromat/.

50 **While a Moldovan businessman:** Luke Harding, "The Global Laundromat: How Did It Work and Who Benefited?," *Guardian*, March 20, 2017. See also the OCCRP's 2021 update: https://www.occrp.org/en/daily/14073-moscow-court-sentences-banker-in-russian-laundromat-case.

50 **When oligarchs are caught:** For example, Piotr Smolar, "The US Is Fight-

ing the Other 'War' Against Russia Through Offshore Accounts, Villas and Yachts," *Le Monde*, January 29, 2023.

50 **Putin himself exemplifies this:** "Putin's Asymmetric Assault on Democracy in Russia and Europe," https://www.govinfo.gov/content/pkg/CPRT -115SPRT28110/html/CPRT-115SPRT28110.htm.

51 **Adherents to that ideology:** Craib, *Adventure Capitalism*, 5.

51 **Offshore is a refuge:** For more on this, see Craib, *Adventure Capitalism*, and Slobodian, *Crack-Up Capitalism*.

51 **"Onerously high, *some may say unethical*":** The STEP textbook quotation is from Michael Parkinson and Dai Jones, *Trust Administration and Accounts* (Birmingham, UK: Central Law Training, 2008), 267.

52 **"Its bugbears are government":** Nicholas Shaxson, *Treasure Islands: Tax Havens and the Men Who Stole the World* (New York: Macmillan, 2014), 185.

52 **Adherents of this worldview:** See Hans-Hermann Hoppe, *Democracy: The God That Failed* (New Brunswick, NJ: Transaction Publishers, 2001), especially p. 211.

52 **For example, Peter Thiel:** George Monbiot, "Our Economic Ruin Means Freedom for the Super-Rich," *Guardian*, July 30, 2012.

52 **This includes not just anti-corruption:** Will Fitzgibbon, "As Kenyan President Mounted Anti-Corruption Comeback, His Family's Secret Fortune Expanded Offshore," International Consortium of Investigative Journalists, October 3, 2021.

53 **"The 1920s were the":** Peter Thiel, "The Education of a Libertarian," Cato Institute, April 13, 2009; https://www.cato-unbound.org/2009/04/13/ peter-thiel/education-libertarian/.

54 **While Mercer himself has:** Quoted in Jane Mayer, "The Reclusive Hedge Fund Tycoon Behind the Trump Presidency," *New Yorker*, March 17, 2017.

54 **The global convergence in:** Bruno Cousin and Sébastien Chauvin, "Is There a Global Super-Bourgeoisie?" *Sociology Compass* 15 (2021).

54 **The financial services industry:** The phrase was made famous in a 2005 note to Citigroup investors by financial analyst Ajay Kapur and colleagues Niall MacLeod and Narendra Singh: https://delong.typepad.com/ plutonomy-1.pdf.

55 **For one thing, they:** On elite sociability and residence in shared communities, see Michael Useem, *The Inner Circle* (New York: Oxford University Press, 1984). On intermarriage and elite sociability, see Michel Pinçon and Monique Pinçon-Charlot, *Grand Fortunes: Dynasties of Wealth in France* (New York: Algora Publishing, 1998).

56   **"You see the same people":** Quoted in Chrystia Freeland, "The Rise of the New Global Elite," *Atlantic*, January–February 2011.

56   **This goes beyond the crackpots:** Rozina Sabur, "US Tech Mogul Using 17-Year-Old Son's Blood in Effort to Stay Young," *Telegraph*, May 23, 2023.

57   **which Thiel listed:** "Peter Thiel's 6 Favorite Books That Predict the Future," *The Week*, May 2, 2016.

57   **"Commanding vastly greater resources":** James Dale Davidson and William Rees-Mogg, *The Sovereign Individual* (London: Macmillan, 1997), 20.

CHAPTER 3: ZOMBIE COLONIALISM

58   **The city's temple to:** The Incas financed such ambitious building projects with a tax system so ruthlessly efficient that even the poorest members of society were required to hand over whatever they had to imperial tax collectors—including the lice on their bodies. These and other details on the administration of the Inca Empire can be found in the *Comentarios Reales de los Incas* (1609) by Garcilaso de la Vega, a direct descendant of the Inca royal family of Cusco and the first published mestizo author of colonial South America. Full text in English translation here: https://quod.lib .umich.edu/e/eebo/A42257.0001.001/1:9?rgn=div1;view=fulltext.

59   **Economist Ronen Palan estimates:** Ronen Palan, "The Second British Empire and the Re-emergence of Global Finance," in *Legacies of Empire: Imperial Roots of the Contemporary Global Order*, ed. Sandra Halperin and Ronen Palan (Cambridge: Cambridge University Press, 2015), 46–68.

59   **It's an operating system:** Elizabeth Paton, "Sexy Fish Caters to London's Stateless Super-Rich," *New York Times*, December 13, 2015.

59   **"While colonialism in its formal sense":** Robin D. G. Kelley, "A Poetics of Anticolonialism," introduction to Aimé Césaire, *Discourse on Colonialism*, trans. Joan Pinkham (1950; repr., New York: Monthly Review Press, 2000), 27.

59   **Though empires come and go:** For an excellent discussion of Marx as a gothic horror novelist turned political economist, see Ann Cvetkovich, *Mixed Feelings: Feminism, Mass Culture, and Victorian Sensationalism* (New Brunswick, NJ: Rutgers University Press, 1992). Marx repeatedly describes the operations of capitalism as vampire-like in *Das Kapital*; it is thought that his inspiration for this insight may have been the eighteenth-century German folktales concerning vampires and a classic short story of Gothic

literature, "The Vampyre," by John Polidori, published just a year after Marx's birth.

60 **Martinican poet Aimé Césaire**: Césaire, *Discourse on Colonialism*, 76.

60 **A rogues' gallery of:** For an excellent history of the competition between British and American banks for economic control of the Caribbean region, see Peter Hudson, *Bankers and Empire: How Wall Street Colonized the Caribbean* (Chicago: University of Chicago Press, 2017).

60 **The Spanish, after all:** The city of Tangiers was a short-lived exception: after being under both Spanish and French rule, it became an international tax-free zone in the mid-twentieth century, until its legal incorporation into Morocco in 1956. For a short account, see Vanessa Ogle, "'Funk Money': The End of Empires, the Expansion of Tax Havens, and Decolonisation as an Economic and Financial Event," *Past & Present* 249, no. 1 (2020): 213–49.

61 **"It is the protections that tax havens":** Koram, *Uncommon Wealth*, 186.

61 **What tax burden existed:** For more on this, see Koram, *Uncommon Wealth*.

61 **"Few organized governments taxed":** Edwin Perkins, *The Economy of Colonial America* (New York: Columbia University Press, 1988), 187.

62 **Overall, the tax burden:** For data and analysis of taxation in the Spanish colonies, see Alejandra Irigoin, "Representation Without Taxation, Taxation Without Consent: The Legacy of Spanish Colonialism in America," *Revista de Historia Economica—Journal of Iberian and Latin American Economic History* 34 (2016): 169–208.

62 **"privileged site of accumulation":** The phrase is from Greta Krippner, "The Financialization of the American Economy," *Socio-Economic Review* 3 (2005): 173–208.

62 **"manipulating facets of ownership":** Graham Moffat, *Trust Law: Text and Materials* (Cambridge: Cambridge University Press, 2009), 5.

63 **It is now a mainstay:** See chapter 4 of my 2016 book, *Capital Without Borders*, along with this article by Yale Law School professor (emeritus) John Langbein: "The Secret Life of the Trust: The Trust as an Instrument of Commerce," *Yale Law Journal* 107 (1997): 165–89.

63 **Trusts are private agreements:** For a full discussion of trusts—where they come from and how they are used—see my article "Trusts and Financialization," *Socio-Economic Review* 15 (2017): 31–63.

65 **In the words of legal:** Koram, *Uncommon Wealth*, 163.

65 **All that said, the metamorphosis:** For a fuller discussion of this accidental and historically contingent development, see political scientist

Ronen Palan's book *The Offshore World* (Ithaca, NY: Cornell University Press, 2006).

66   **That was a significant burden:** On the £50 travel limit, see this transcript of a 1969 Parliamentary debate: https://api.parliament.uk/historic-hansard/commons/1969/jun/30/foreign-travel-allowance-lb50-limit. On the transfer limit for foreign real estate, see Joseph P. Collins, "British Abolish Controls on Foreign Currency," October 24, 1979.

66   **One could always risk:** Howard Marks's recollections are quoted in Ioan Grillo, "How Howard Marks Helped Revolutionize the Drug Trade," *Time*, April 12, 2016. For Britons caught and fined for attempting to evade currency controls by moving undeclared cash out of the United Kingdom in the 1970s, see Clyde Farnsworth, "Flood of Smuggled Cash Is Enriching Swiss Banks," *New York Times*, May 11, 1976.

66   **As imperial control retreated:** On patterns of colonialism by the Spanish Empire, see Matthew Lange, James Mahoney, and Matthias vom Hau, "Colonialism and Development: A Comparative Analysis of Spanish and British Colonies," *American Journal of Sociology* 111, no. 5 (2006): 1412–62; on German colonial history, see George Steinmetz, "The Colonial State as a Social Field: Ethnographic Capital and Native Policy in the German Overseas Empire Before 1914," *American Sociological Review* 73 (2008): 589–612.

66   **The result, as one sociological:** Lange et al., "Colonialism and Development," 1428.

67   **These included the Bahamas:** See Ogle, "'Funk Money': The End of Empires," for an in-depth discussion.

67   **The Caymans had no:** For an account of this period, see Walker's memoir, *From Georgetown to George Town: A Personal History of William Stuart Walker and His Part in Beginning of the Cayman Islands as an Offshore Financial Center* (Davie, FL: JPSC, 2012).

68   **Turks and Caicos became:** According to the U.S. Bureau of International Narcotics and Law Enforcement Affairs, *International Narcotics Control Strategy Report*, vol. 2: *Money Laundering and Financial Crimes, Turks and Caicos* (Washington, DC: U.S. Department of State, 2014).

68   **After moving to the BVI:** For the "radical," "backwater," and "quasi-religious text" quotes, see Colin Riegels, "The BVI IBC Act and the Building of a Nation," *IFC Review*, March 1, 2014.

69   **Those fees now contribute:** Trevor Cole, "How I Learned to Avoid the Taxman in the British Virgin Islands," *Globe and Mail*, January 27, 2011.

69   **It was a stunning:** The quote comes from Sir Douglas Jardine, former gov-

ernor of several British territories, including Somaliland, Borneo, and the Leeward Islands—a Caribbean chain that includes what is now the British Virgin Islands. His remark appears in his review of *The Virgin Islands*, by Luther H. Evans, *Journal of Comparative Legislation and International Law*, 29, nos. 3–4 (1947): 69.

69 **The country now hosts:** For the 40 percent figure, see Emile van der Does de Willebois, Emily M. Halter, Robert A. Harrison, Ji Won Park, and J. C. Sharman, *The Puppet Masters: How the Corrupt Use Legal Structures to Hide Stolen Assets and What to Do About It* (Washington, DC: World Bank, 2011).

69 **"enjoy a standard of living far higher":** Ibid.

69 **Other aspiring financial centers:** Humphry Leue, "British Virgin Islands: The BVI International Business Company at the Crossroads," *IFC Review*, December 16, 2004.

69 **Within twenty years, the Caymans:** Tony Freyer and Andrew Morriss, "Creating Cayman as an Offshore Financial Center: Structure and Strategy Since 1960," *Arizona State Law Journal* 45 (2013): 1297–1396. See also Steve Lohr, "Where the Money Washes Up," *New York Times*, March 29, 1992.

70 **Queen Elizabeth II made:** For the "economic miracle" quote, see Lohr, "Where the Money Washes Up." For the OBE story, see Walker, *From Georgetown to George Town*.

70 **"the éminence grise":** See the *Telegraph*'s obituary, "Milton Grundy, Lawyer Who Pioneered Offshore Tax Havens and Philanthropist Who Set Up a Gallery in His Own Home for Promising Artists," January 8, 2023.

70 **"the most notorious tax haven":** Jacques Peretti, "The Cayman Islands: Home to 100,000 Companies and the £8.50 Packet of Fish Fingers," *Guardian*, January 18, 2016.

71 **"as a means for territories":** Raymond Craib, *Adventure Capitalism: A History of Libertarian Exit, from the Era of Decolonization to the Digital Age* (Oakland, CA: PM Press, 2022), 93.

71 **When Ponce de León:** Richard Oulahan and William Lambert, "The Scandal in the Bahamas," *Life*, February 3, 1967, 64.

71 **"primitive and rustic":** The quotation is from the early history of the island as recounted by the Grand Bahama Museum in the section "A Wilderness Tamed."

71 **pro-monarchy and pro-Confederacy Americans:** Craib, *Adventure Capitalism*, 95.

72 **First, Canadians discovered that:** For a brief historical review, see Ralph Deans, "History and Success—Financial Services Evolution," *Bahamas Investor Magazine*, June 23, 2009.

72 **In the 1860s, Nassau:** Oulahan and Lambert, "The Scandal in the Bahamas," 65.

73 **This turned out to be:** Both quotes are from Deans, "History and Success."

73 **Setting a precedent for:** The term was coined by University of Oxford law professor Doreen McBarnet in "Legitimate Rackets: Tax Evasion, Tax Avoidance, and the Boundaries of Legality," *Journal of Human Justice*, 3 (1992): 56–74.

73 **And, legend has it:** Brandan Adams, "The Real McCoy," Mariners' Museum and Park, November 14, 2022.

73 **This tradition of using the:** For a brief history, see Joseph Thorndike, "In the 1930s, the Bahamas Became a Tax Problem for the Treasury," *Forbes*, June 24, 2021.

73 **Because of laws designed:** Craib, *Adventure Capitalism*, 93. See also Anthony Audley Thompson, *An Economic History of the Bahamas* (Nassau, Bahamas: Commonwealth Publications, 1979).

74 **"Another factor was the secrecy":** Thompson, *An Economic History of the Bahamas*, 82.

75 **Aimé Césaire soon recognized:** Césaire, *Discourse on Colonialism*, 76.

75 **In keeping with this pattern:** On Canadian Louis Chesler and his Mafia links, see "The Charges Against Resorts," *New York Times*, March 4, 1979. On Swiss banker and Devil's Island escapee Alber Leschevin, see this brief record from the Grand Bahama Museum: https://www.grandbahamamuseum.org/lives-lived/alber-leschevin.

75 **Eventually, organized crime moved:** See Oulahan and Lambert, "The Scandal in the Bahamas," 64.

75 **"surrender of sovereignty":** The quotation is from Michael Craton and Gail Saunders's magisterial *Islanders in the Stream: A History of the Bahamian People*, vol. 2, *From the Ending of Slavery to the Twenty-First Century* (Athens: University of Georgia Press, 2011), 324. For more on the seizure of sovereignty as a defining event in colonization, see Steinmetz, "The Colonial State as a Social Field."

75 **As an exposé in *Life*:** Oulahan and Lambert, "The Scandal in the Bahamas," 69.

76 **His project was thus:** Steven Press, *Rogue Empires* (Cambridge, MA: Harvard University Press, 2017).

76 **True to type, Groves:** Robert Reno, "Suit Challenges Bahamas Land Title," *Miami Herald*, December 20, 1967.

76 *Life* **likened the arrangement:** Oulahan and Lambert, "The Scandal in the Bahamas," 69. For a brief history of the East India Company and its role in building the British Empire, see Emily Erikson and Peter Bearman, "Malfeasance and the Foundations for Global Trade: The Structure of English Trade in the East Indies," *American Journal of Sociology* 112, no. 1 (2006): 195–230.

76 **That included the racialized:** Craig Wolff, "Wallace Groves Is Dead at 86; Developer of Resort in Bahamas," obituary, *New York Times*, February 1, 1988.

76 **As the historians of the Grand:** For a recap of this history, illustrated with primary source documents, see the website of the Grand Bahama Museum and the section "Creation of the Grand Bahama Port Authority."

77 **Within fifteen years of the:** Tony Doggart, *Tax Havens and Offshore Funds* (London: Economist Intelligence Unit, 1971), 44.

77 **Local publications billed it:** From the biannual trade and tourist publication *What to Do: Nassau, Freeport* (Nassau: E. Dupuch Publications, July–December 1975), 4.

77 **Hundreds of American, Canadian:** For the 85 percent figure, see "The Trust Companies," *Bahamas Handbook and Businessman's Annual, 1975–76* (Nassau: Etienne Dupuch, Jr., Publications, 1975). For the data points in the rest of the sentence, see "Financial Survey of the Bahamas Now: An Interview with the Governor of the Bahamas Central Bank," *Bahamian Review* 23, nos. 11–12 (November–December 1975).

77 **Thus, two years after:** See *Bahamian Review* 23, nos. 11–12 (November–December 1975): 11.

78 **"Some of the methods employed":** Oliver Gibson, "A Guide to the Bahamas as a Leading Tax Haven," *Bahamas Handbook and Businessman's Annual, 1978–79* (Nassau: Dupuch Publications), 199.

78 **As a "freelance imperialist":** For other examples of "freelance imperialists," see Hudson, *Bankers and Empire*, and Craib, *Adventure Capitalism*.

78 **"the richest country in the Caribbean":** Jessie Williams, "Five Reasons to Live in the Bahamas," *Financial Times*, January 13, 2019. For the 20 percent figure, see Deans, "History and Success."

78 **These figures represent an:** From *Race and Class in the Colonial Bahamas, 1880–1960* (Gainesville: University Press of Florida, 2016), by the islands' premier historian, Gail Saunders.

79   **This extreme economic vulnerability:** As detailed in Craib, *Adventure Capitalism.*

79   **"intrepid developer Wallace Groves":** William Cartwright, "Letter from the Editor: Royal Recognition for Freeport," *Bahamian Review* 7, no. 7 (July–August 1965), 4; https://www.grandbahamamuseum.org/images/pdfs/gbm-bahamian-review-vol7-no7-jul-aug-1965.pdf.

79   **In fact, by the late:** "Investors Watching Bahamas Will Suit," *Fort Lauderdale News*, December 20, 1967. Full text here: https://bahamianology.com/savaletta-hanna-forged-will-of-black-illiterate-poor-farmer-and-land-you-know-how-it-ends-freeport-1967/.

79   **The result has been:** Gordon Lewis, *The Growth of the Modern West Indies* (Kingston, Jamaica: Ian Randle Publishers, 2004), 337.

79   **Soon afterward, he was knighted:** For details on Brooke, see Press, *Rogue Empires.* For more on Labuan, see Mia Lamar, "The Tiny Malaysian Island That Wants to Be a Tax Haven," *Wall Street Journal*, June 2, 2016.

CHAPTER 4: THE PARADOX OF PLENTY

80   **In the early 1990s:** See, for example, Richard Auty, *Sustaining Development in Mineral Economies: The Resource Curse Thesis* (New York: Routledge, 1993).

80   **Terry Karl, a Stanford:** Terry Karl, *The Paradox of Plenty: Oil Booms and Petro-States* (Berkeley: University of California Press, 1997).

81   **Precipitous economic, political, and social:** See Nick Shaxson, *The Finance Curse: How Global Finance Is Making Us All Poorer* (New York: Grove, 2019).

81   **"Despite the appearance that":** Kojo Koram, *Uncommon Wealth: Britain and the Aftermath of Empire* (London: John Murray, 2022), 186.

82   **"Those in power battle":** Oliver Bullough, *Butler to the World* (London: Profile Books, 2022), 155.

83   **When the most powerful:** In an article for the *Atlantic*, I expanded on the idea of "aspirational impunity" in the American context: "Trump's Very Ordinary Indifference to the Common Good," October 10, 2020.

83   **One former wealth manager:** Nicholas Shaxson, "The Truth About Tax Havens," *Guardian*, January 8, 2011.

83   **Bahamian firm Harry B. Sands:** All quoted characterizations of the firm Harry B. Sands, Lobosky & Company can be found on the home page of the firm's website: www.hbslaw.com. All quoted characterizations of firm founder Harry B. Sands can be found under the subheading of the firm's

website titled "Tribute: Harry B. Sands": www.hbslaw.com/about-the
-practice/tribute-harry-b-sands.

83   **Former Swiss banker turned:** Both the Bahamas "concrete shoes" story and
the Swiss whistleblower reports are from Shaxson, "The Truth About Tax
Havens."

84   **"It is damaging our":** Jerome Taylor and Peter Bild, *Independent*,
"WikiLeaks to 'Disclose Tax Dodge Files,'" *Independent*, January 17,
2011.

84   **The bank denied any:** See Shaxson, "The Truth About Tax Havens."

84   **As one longtime Maltese:** Jon Wertheim, "Inside the Corruption Allegations Plaguing Malta," *60 Minutes*, August 16, 2020.

84   **Caruana Galizia was assassinated:** From Daphne Caruana Galizia's note-
book blog *Running Commentary*, dated October 16, 2017, and titled "That
Crook Schembri Was in Court Today, Pleading That He Is Not a Crook."

84   **After two of his close:** Oren Gruenbaum, "Malta: Muscat Resigns After
Protests over Caruana Galizia Assassination," *Roundtable: The Commonwealth Journal of Current Affairs*, January 20, 2020.

84   **One retiree told the:** Alexander Clapp, "The Prime Minister and the Mur-
dered Journalist: Inside Malta, a Nation on the Brink," *Economist*, December 11, 2019.

86   **Not an ideal environment:** Pritish Behuria, "The Political Economy of a
Tax Haven: The Case of Mauritius," *Review of International Political Economy* 30, no. 2 (2022): 772–800.

87   **In fact, shortly after I left:** U.S. Department of State, *2017 Country Reports
on Human Rights Practices: Mauritius*, https://www.state.gov/reports/2017
-country-reports-on-human-rights-practices/mauritius/. See also Jean Paul
Arouff, "Mauritius Police Search Journalists' Homes After Money Laundering Story," Reuters, September 25, 2017.

87   **Enough of that wealth:** Will Fitzgibbon, "Tax Haven Mauritius' Rise
Comes at the Rest of Africa's Expense," International Consortium of Investigative Journalists, December 7, 2017.

88   **After the Paradise Papers:** Ibid.

88   **The country had been transformed:** Colin Riegels, "The BVI IBC Act and
the Building of a Nation," *IFC Review*, March 1, 2014.

88   **With so many "businessmen":** As recounted by one of the wealth managers I interviewed, who worked there; see my book *Capital Without Borders*
(Cambridge, MA: Harvard University Press, 2016), 139.

89   **The commission's report not only:** Melanie Paulick, "British Virgin Islands

Governor Begins Corruption Inquiry with Support of UK," *Jurist*, January 20, 2021.

89 **The commission concluded its:** Tahira Mohamedbhai, "Report Reveals British Virgin Islands Government Corruption, Suggests Constitutional Suspension," *Jurist*, April 30, 2021.

89 **A year after the:** Vimal Patel, "Premier of British Virgin Islands Arrested on Drug Trafficking Charges in U.S.," *New York Times*, April 28, 2022.

90 **That the article's *subtitle*:** The full title was "Trust and Estate Planning: The Emergence of a Profession and Its Contribution to Socioeconomic Inequality"; it appeared in *Sociological Forum* 27 (2012): 825–46.

91 **She was investigating allegations:** See Steven Morris, "How 'House of Horror' Investigation Brought Jersey Abuse to Light," *Guardian*, July 3, 2017.

91 **Other journalists had begun:** See Bullough, *Butler to the World*, for a summary of the earlier reporting prior to Goodman's arrival.

92 **Jersey's own chief of:** Helen Pidd, "Jersey's 'Secrecy Culture' Led to My Suspension, Says Former Police Chief," *Guardian*, June 12, 2012.

92 **Similarly, Jersey's former health:** See a contemporaneous news story by Jerome Taylor, "MP Gives Asylum to Jersey Whistle-Blower," *Independent*, October 26, 2009.

92 **By the time Goodman:** The story, as relayed by Goodman and reported in numerous outlets, is quite a remarkable testament to the power of the offshore financial services industry: https://leahmcgrathgoodman.com/anarchy-in-the-uk/.

94 **Referring to a recent:** For the scandal, see "Deals Dishonour the Country," *Cook Islands News*, July 19, 2013.

95 **This way of reframing:** See Anthony van Fossen, "Money Laundering, Global Financial Instability, and Tax Havens in the Pacific Islands," *Contemporary Pacific* 15 (2003): 237–75, especially p. 259.

96 **The contrast between the:** Sophie Kesteven, "El Chorrillo Bears the Scars of a US Invasion and Gang Violence, but Amid the Heartache, There's Hope," Australian Broadcasting Corporation, May 22, 2020.

96 **Its economy has been booming:** Cristina Guevara, "In Panama, Protesters Want Deeper Reform," *Americas Quarterly*, August 1, 2002.

96 **The financial services industry catering:** According to analysis of 2019 data from the U.S. Securities and Exchange Commission: https://www.sec.gov/Archives/edgar/data/76027/000119312520249543/d20553dex99d.htm.

96   **But according to World Bank:** As reported in Marcelo Justo, "¿Cuáles Son los 6 Países Más Desiguales de América Latina?," BBC Mundo, March 9, 2016.

96   **The country's Indigenous people:** Stephanie Ott, "Worlds Apart: Panama's Indigenous and the Panama Papers," Al Jazeera, April 9, 2016.

96   **Roberto Eisenmann:** Quoted in Jason Beaubien, "Panama Booms While Poor Watch from Afar," *All Things Considered*, NPR, April 16, 2012.

97   **Virtually all the elites:** Tracy Wilkinson, "Skilled Foreigners Flood Panama, Leaving Many Residents Without Jobs," *Los Angeles Times*, June 19, 2015.

97   **Panama City ranks number eight:** Nick Van Mead and Jo Blason, "The Ten World Cities with the Highest Murder Rates—in Pictures," *Guardian*, June 24, 2014.

97   **The United Kingdom itself, long:** Koram, *Uncommon Wealth*, 5.

97   **At the same time:** See David Davis, "Democracy Is at Risk; We Can't Let Oligarchs Exploit British Courts to Silence Their Critics," *Guardian*, November 29, 2022.

97   **"Putin's cronies," she said:** Home Secretary Priti Patel's speech to Parliament was quoted in "Patel Criticises 'Gangster' Putin as MPs Rush Through Economic Crime Laws," *Standard*, March 7, 2022.

97   **Shortly afterward, a Conservative:** Bullough, *Butler to the World*, xv.

98   **So much so that journalist:** Bullough discusses these tours in his book *Moneyland* (New York: St. Martin's, 2019), as well as in this 2019 interview with Terry Gross on the NPR show *Fresh Air*: https://www.npr.org/2019/05/01/719001286/moneyland-reveals-how-oligarchs-kleptocrats-and-crooks-stash-fortunes.

98   **This has driven up:** Yustina Baltrusyte, "Foreign Ownership Is on the Rise and Driving Up Housing Prices," *The Developer*, December 20, 2021.

98   **At the same time, they're:** The U.K. "stamp tax" (real estate sales tax) dodge, which figured prominently in the offshore data leaked in the 2017 Paradise Papers, was detailed in James Ball, "Secret Film Shows How Buyers of Luxury London Homes Can Avoid Millions in Tax," *Guardian*, December 16, 2012.

99   **Not only did the United Kingdom's:** Koram, *Uncommon Wealth*, 184.

99   **For example, while one part:** Lauren Tara LaCapra, "Goldman Lowered Tax Bill by 10 Mln Pounds—Report," Reuters, October 12, 2011.

99   **Thanks to its robust:** For the figures on Luxembourg, see this 2021 "Facts and Figures" sheet from EIS Finanzplatz: https://www.eisfinanzplaz.lu/en/view/facts-figures/.

For the 2021 per capita GDP figure, see Eurostat: https://ec.europa
.eu/eurostat/statistics-explained/index.php?title=GDP_per_capita,_
consumption_per_capita_and_price_level_indices.

99 **However, according to economist:** Gabriel Zucman, *The Hidden Wealth of
Nations* (Chicago: University of Chicago Press, 2015).

99 **Almost 60 percent of:** See this December 2022 report by Research Luxembourg, based on Eurostat figures: https://www.researchluxembourg.org/
en/luxembourg-has-the-highest-proportion-of-foreign-born-residents-in
-europe/.

99 **"The situation," Zucman writes:** Zucman, *Hidden Wealth of Nations*,
88–89.

100 **But having "sold its sovereignty":** Zucman, *Hidden Wealth of Nations*,
87–88.

100 **Locals are also hit:** See Oliver Bullough, "The Fall of Jersey: How a Tax
Haven Goes Bust," *Guardian*, December 8, 2015, for example.

101 **"There is no economic":** Patrick Wintour, "Tax Havens Have No Economic Justification, Say Top Economists," *Guardian*, May 9, 2016.

102 **But since the discovery:** Scott Pegg, "Has Botswana Beaten the Resource
Curse?," in *Mineral Rents and the Financing of Social Policy: Opportunities and
Challenges*, ed. Katja Hujo (London: Palgrave Macmillan, 2012), 257–84.

102 **Among the keys to:** Paula Meijia and Vincent Castel, "Could Oil Shine
Like Diamonds?," *African Development Bank Economic Brief*, October 2012.

102 **Maybe the economist Jeffrey Sachs:** See Wintour, "Tax Havens Have No
Economic Justification."

CHAPTER 5: THIS SIDE OF FISCAL PARADISE

103 **In *The Great Gatsby*:** F. Scott Fitzgerald, *The Great Gatsby* (1925; repr., New
York: Simon & Schuster, 1992), 8.

103 **That is, "power is not":** C. Wright Mills, *The Power Elite* (New York: Oxford
University Press, 1956), 11.

104 **The impacts are felt:** Jason Sharman, *Havens in a Storm: The Struggle for
Global Tax Regulation* (Ithaca, NY: Cornell University Press, 2006).

105 **In the short term:** Tom Phillips, "High Above Sao Paulo's Choked Streets,
the Rich Cruise a New Highway," *Guardian*, June 20, 2008.

105 **In the long term:** Evan Osnos, "Doomsday Prep for the Super Rich," *New
Yorker*, January 23, 2017. See also Sheila Marikar, "The Rich Are Planning
to Leave This Wretched Planet," *New York Times*, June 10, 2018.

105 **For now, content to:** See, for example, my *New York Times* op-ed "Trump's Tax Avoidance Is a Tax on the Rest of Us," October 1, 2020, A27.

105 **They need only to fill:** This idea is from Bruno Latour, *Down to Earth: Politics in the New Climactic Regime*, trans. Catherine Porter (Cambridge: Polity, 2018).

106 **Doomsday and mass death:** Douglas Rushkoff, *Survival of the Richest: Escape Fantasies of the Tech Billionaires* (New York: W. W. Norton, 2022).

106 **Sometimes, these conditions are:** Kojo Koram, *Uncommon Wealth: Britain and the Aftermath of Empire* (London: John Murray, 2022).

106 **A growing body of research:** On adult suicide rates as a result of austerity policies, see Veronica Toffolutti and Marc Suhrcke, "Does Austerity Really Kill?," *Economics and Human Biology* 33 (2019): 211–23. See also Nikolaos Antonakakis and Alan Collins, "The Impact of Fiscal Austerity on Suicide: On the Empirics of a Modern Greek Tragedy," *Social Science & Medicine* 112 (2014): 39–50. On infant mortality rates as a result of austerity policies, see Rajmil Luis, David Taylor-Robinson, Geir Gunnlaugsson, Anders Hjern, and Nick Spencer, "Trends in Social Determinants of Child Health and Perinatal Outcomes in European Countries 2005–2015 by Level of Austerity Imposed by Governments: A Repeat Cross-Sectional Analysis of Routinely Available Data," *BMJ Open* 8, no. 10 (2018): e022932.

107 **Social murder, he wrote:** Friedrich Engels, *The Condition of the Working Class in England* (1845; repr., London: Oxford University Press, 2009).

107 **There was nothing hidden:** Stafford Poole, " 'War by Fire and Blood': The Church and the Chichimecas 1585," *The Americas* 22 (1965): 115–37.

108 **This is where offshore intersects:** Thomas Piketty, "Foreword," in Gabriel Zucman, *The Hidden Wealth of Nations* (Chicago: University of Chicago Press, 2015), and Ruth Ben-Ghiat, *Strongmen: Mussolini to the Present* (New York: W. W. Norton, 2020).

108 **"war of all against all":** The famous phrase originates with the English political philosopher Thomas Hobbes and his 1651 book on the purpose of government, *Leviathan, or The Matter, Forme and Power of a Commonwealth Ecclesiasticall and Civil.*

109 **Tolstoy, who was a:** *What Then Must We Do?*, trans. Aylmer Maude (London: Geoffrey Cumberlege / Oxford University Press, 1925), and "Need It Be So?" in Lev N. Tolstóy, *Miscellaneous Letters and Essays*, vol. 23 of *The Complete Works of Count Tolstoy*, trans. Leo Wiener (Boston: Dana Estes, 1905). Tolstoy attempted to free his serfs during his lifetime, but they refused, suspecting that they were being tricked into a bad deal. Instead, after his death,

Tolstoy's wife and children transferred ownership of the family land to the serfs. See Hilde Hoogenboom, "Estate Culture and Yasnaya Polyana," in *Tolstoy in Context*, ed. Anna Berman (Cambridge: Cambridge University Press, 2022), 28–36. For a very readable introduction to Tolstoy's essays on inequality, see Liza Knapp, *Tolstoy: A Very Short Introduction* (New York: Oxford University Press, 2019).

109   **What's needed is not:** The phrase originates with Zine Magubane, "Overlapping Territories and Intertwined Histories: Historical Sociology's Global Imagination," in *Remaking Modernity: Politics, History, Sociology*, ed. Julia Adams, Elisabeth Clemens, and Anne Shola (Durham, NC: Duke University Press, 2005), 92–108.

110   **Unfortunately, his bill died:** I am indebted for this story to Oliver Bullough, who recounts it in *Butler to the World* (London: Profile Books, 2022), 84.

110   **This collaboration significantly reduced:** Adam Hofri-Winogradow, "Professionals' Contribution to the Legislative Process: Between Self, Client and the Public," *Law and Social Inquiry* 39 (2014): 96–126.

111   **We demonstrated that when:** Ho-Chun Herbert Chang, Brooke Harrington, Feng Fu, and Daniel Rockmore, "Complex Systems of Secrecy," *PNAS Nexus* 2 (2023): 1–12.

111   **Sharing the secrets of:** See my 2016 book, *Capital Without Borders* (Cambridge, MA: Harvard University Press, 2016), particularly p. 147.

111   **The same principle obtains:** Diego Gambetta, "Mafia: The Price of Distrust," in *Trust: Making and Breaking Cooperative Relations*, ed. Diego Gambetta (New York: Basil Blackwell, 1988), 158–75.

112   **At least twenty:** Sara Ruberg and Max Colchester, "Roman Abramovich, Other Sanctioned Russian Oligarchs Fight Back in Court," *Wall Street Journal*, July 16, 2022.

113   **As one Swiss wealth:** See my book *Capital Without Borders*, 69.

113   **The policy tradition of:** Mollie McGowan, "Between a Rock and a Hard Place: The Export of Technical Data Under the International Traffic in Arms Regulations," *George Washington Law Review* 76 (2008): 1327–41.

114   **"could not access its foreign":** Kenneth Katzmann, "Iran Sanctions," Congressional Research Service Report RS20871, February 2, 2002; https://crsreports.congress.gov/product/pdf/RS/RS20871/315. See also Carla E. Humud and Clayton Thomas, "Iran Sanctions," Congressional Research Service Report RS20871, February 2, 2002; https://crsreports.congress.gov/product/pdf/RS/RS20871/317.

114   **The prospect that cooperation:** For the $100 to $150 billion figure, see

Suzanne Maloney, "Sanctions and the Iranian Nuclear Deal: Silver Bullet or Blunt Object?," *Social Research* 82, no. 4 (2015): 887–911.

114 **Recently, a court in Geneva:** Nick Cumming-Bruce, "Bankers Are Convicted of Allowing a Putin Ally to Deposit Millions in Swiss Accounts," *New York Times*, March 30, 2023.

114 **The United States has also banned:** Neil Amato, "US Sanctions Ban Provision of Accounting, Consulting Services to Russia," *Journal of Accounting Research*, May 9, 2022.

114 **The European Union and the United Kingdom:** "Press Statement by President von der Leyen on a New Package of Restrictive Measures Against Russia," European Commission, September 28, 2022. See also "Sanctions in Response to Putin's Illegal Annexation of Ukrainian Regions," U.K. Foreign and Commonwealth Development Office, September 30, 2022.

115 **Even Cyprus—so dependent:** Louis Ashworth, "Why Cyprus Is a 'Russian Bank with Dirty Money Posing as an E.U. State,'" *Telegraph*, March 2, 2022. See also Merve Berker, "Russian Warships Denied Berth in Southern Cyprus," Anadolu Agency, March 5, 2022.

115 **Singapore stopped short of:** Philip Heijmans, "Singapore to Sanction Russia in 'Almost Unprecedented' Move," Bloomberg, February 28, 2022.

115 **For decades, offshore centers:** See Kalyeena Makortoff, "How Swiss Banking Secrecy Enabled an Unequal Global Financial System," *Guardian*, February 22, 2022. See also Oliver Bullough, "Nevis: How the World's Most Secretive Offshore Haven Refuses to Clean Up," *Guardian*, July 12, 2018.

117 **Hence his stark conclusion:** Pliny, *Natural History*, vol. 5, trans. H. Rackham, Loeb Classical Library 371 (Cambridge, MA: Harvard University Press, 1950), book 18.

117 **The resemblance extends even:** For a detailed review of the Romans' view of the *latifundia* system and its impact on their society, see Vladimir Simkhovitch, "Rome's Fall Reconsidered," *Political Science Quarterly* 31 (1916): 201–43; my synthesis is particularly reliant on information on pp. 202 and 206.

119 **Even the monthly magazine:** J. Riches, "The New Boundaries," *STEP Journal*, November 2012.

119 **The power of shame:** See HM Revenue & Customs Research Report 537, "Researching the Drivers of Tax Compliance Behaviour Among the Wealthy and Ways to Improve It," January 2019.

119 **This fear of socio-emotional:** See, for example: BBC, "UK Vows to Stop the Super-Rich Using Courts to Silence Critics," March 17, 2022.

.

READINGS IN CONVERSATION

GENERAL ACADEMIC SOURCES FOR *OFFSHORE*

Bullough, Oliver. *Moneyland: The Inside Story of the Crooks and Kleptocrats Who Rule the World*. New York: St. Martin's, 2019.
Everything Bullough—a journalist specializing in the post-Soviet world—has written about offshore is extremely valuable, but this offers a particularly wide-ranging view. His 2022 follow-up, *Butler to the World*, is also very informative about the imperial origins of offshore finance.

Harrington, Brooke. *Capital Without Borders: Wealth Managers and the One Percent*. Cambridge, MA: Harvard University Press, 2016.
This, my first book on offshore finance, introduces readers to the detailed inner workings of the system; it offers more technical and ethnographic detail on the way offshore finance works legally, socially, and politically.

Hoang, Kimberly Kay. *Spiderweb Capitalism*. Princeton, NJ: Princeton University Press, 2022.
This is an in-depth look at the uses of offshore finance to invest in "frontier markets" throughout less-developed parts of Asia, such as Myanmar, for the benefit of elites in the financial metropoles of Hong Kong and Singapore.

Palan, Ronen, Richard Murphy, and Christian Chavagneux. *Tax Havens: How Globalization Really Works*. Ithaca, NY: Cornell University Press, 2010.
This book explains the overall political economy of the offshore system; it offers a "big picture" view.

Sharman, Jason. *Havens in a Storm: The Struggle for Global Tax Regulation*. Ithaca, NY: Cornell University Press, 2006.
This fascinating book shows how a group of small offshore financial centers successfully rebuffed pressure from large international organizations like the OECD by claiming that regulation represented repression by former imperial powers.

Shaxson, Nicholas. *Treasure Islands: Tax Havens and the Men Who Stole the World*. New York: Macmillan, 2014.
This book, by British journalist Shaxson, was one of the first accounts to grasp the political as well as the economic consequences of offshore finance for the world.

Surak, Kristin. *The Golden Passport: Global Mobility for Millionaires*. Cambridge, MA: Harvard University Press, 2023.
This book offers unique insight on the geographical hypermobility of the ultra-rich—and their wealth—which makes them difficult to constrain in any legal system.

Van Maanen, John. *Tales of the Field: On Writing Ethnography*. Chicago: University of Chicago Press, 1988.
This book elaborates on the methodology of immersion ethnography and its challenges.

Winters, Jeffrey. *Oligarchy*. New York: Cambridge University Press, 2011.
This study of political and economic elites covers ancient Greece to the Mafia, acknowledging the key role of offshore finance in modern cases like the "Civil Oligarchy" of the United States.

Zucman, Gabriel. *The Hidden Wealth of Nations*. Chicago: University of Chicago Press, 2015.
This short book by the leading U.S. economist offers some of the most reliable estimates available on the scope of the financial drain created by offshore finance.

CHAPTER 1: THE UNAUTHORIZED BIOGRAPHY OF A SECRETIVE SYSTEM

Galaz, Victor, et al. "Tax Havens and Global Environmental Degradation." *Nature Ecology & Evolution* (2018) 2: 1352–57.
This was the seminal article on the uses of offshore finance to destroy the environment: in this case, the Amazonian rainforest.

Harrington, Brooke. "Turning Vice into Virtue: Institutional Work and Professional Misconduct." *Human Relations* (2018) 72: 1464–96.
This article provides insight into the way wealth managers understand their work and handle the moral dilemmas of making the rich richer at the expense of everyone else.

Simmel, Georg. *The Sociology of Georg Simmel.* Translated and edited by Kurt H. Wolff. Glencoe, IL: Free Press, 1950.
This compilation of Simmel's most famous essays includes two referenced in this chapter: the one on "the stranger" and the other on "secrecy and secret societies."

CHAPTER 2: A PLATFORM FOR ELITE INSURGENCY

Craib, Raymond. *Adventure Capitalism: A History of Libertarian Exit, from the Era of Decolonization to the Digital Age.* Oakland, CA: PM Press, 2022.
This work of history vividly captures and documents the ragtag band of libertarian anarchists who founded and have benefited from offshore financial centers over the past fifty years.

Gilman, Nils. "The Twin Insurgency." *American Interest* 9, no. 6 (2014).
This brief, seminal article encapsulates the political economy of the global elite insurgency better than any other resource I've encountered. It's a must-read.

Hanna, Mark. *Pirate Nests and the Rise of the British Empire, 1570–1740.* Chapel Hill: University of North Carolina Press, 2017.
This is a wonderfully readable history of the political economy of piracy—an important resource for understanding the origins of modern offshore finance.

Mears, Ashley. *Very Important People.* Princeton, NJ: Princeton University Press, 2020.
This immersion ethnography of the global party circuit offers unique insight on elite sociability.

Mills, C. Wright. *The Power Elite.* New York: Oxford University Press, 1956.
This sociological classic remains highly relevant to understanding present-day elites using the offshore financial system.

Page, Benjamin, Jason Seawright, and Matthew Lacombe. *Billionaires and Stealth Politics*. Chicago: University of Chicago Press, 2019.
In this book, political scientists Page, Seawright, and Lacombe examine the hidden ways that billionaires shape American democracy; this serves as a detailed case study of the global elite insurgency outlined in this chapter.

Slobodian, Quinn. *Crack-Up Capitalism: Market Radicals and the Dream of a World Without Democracy*. New York: Metropolitan Books, 2023.
This historical account provides context for the elite insurgency occurring offshore.

CHAPTER 3: ZOMBIE COLONIALISM

Césaire, Aimé. *Discourse on Colonialism*. Translated by Joan Pinkham. 1950. Reprint, New York: Monthly Review Press, 2000.
This essay is a must-read analysis of colonialism's legacy, filled with remarkably prescient insights relevant to the rise of offshore finance.

Craton, Michael, and Gail Saunders. *Islanders in the Stream: A History of the Bahamian People*. Vol. 2, *From the Ending of Slavery to the Twenty-First Century*. Athens: University of Georgia Press, 2011.
This book is considered the definitive history of the Bahamas, including the circumstances that led to the country's domination by Wallace Groves and offshore finance.

Hudson, Peter. *Bankers and Empire: How Wall Street Colonized the Caribbean*. Chicago: University of Chicago Press, 2017.
This fascinating history details the competition between British and American banks for economic control of the Caribbean region.

Koram, Kojo. *Uncommon Wealth: Britain and the Aftermath of Empire*. London: John Murray, 2022.
This masterful recent book traces the "afterlife" of the British Empire around the world, including in the territories that became offshore financial centers.

Ogle, Vanessa. "'Funk Money': The End of Empires, the Expansion of Tax Havens, and Decolonisation as an Economic and Financial Event." *Past & Present* 249, no. 1 (2020): 213–49.

Ogle is the world's preeminent historian of offshore finance. This article is indispensable to understanding intracolonial capital flight, which made places like the Cayman Islands and the British Virgin Islands centers of offshore activity.

Oulahan, Richard, and William Lambert. "The Scandal in the Bahamas." *Life*, February 3, 1967, 64.
This is the definitive account of the life and work of Wallace Groves, written during his lifetime. It was a feature in the popular national magazine *Life*, with photo illustrations.

Press, Steven. *Rogue Empires*. Cambridge, MA: Harvard University Press, 2017.
This fascinating history of "empire by private contract" tells the story of the buccaneers and pirates who created the template for the offshore financial system.

CHAPTER 4: THE PARADOX OF PLENTY

Harrington, Brooke. "Trust and Estate Planning: A Profession and Its Contribution to Socio-Economic Inequality." *Sociological Forum* 27 (2012): 825–46.
My first publication on offshore finance; this was the piece that led to my confrontation with the BVI wealth manager.

Karl, Terry. *The Paradox of Plenty: Oil Booms and Petro-States*. Berkeley: University of California Press, 1997.
This study in the political economy of development is a key resource for understanding how offshore finance can hollow out the economies and governments of postcolonial societies.

Shaxson, Nicholas. *The Finance Curse: How Global Finance Is Making Us All Poorer*. New York: Grove, 2019.
This follow-up to Shaxson's earlier work on tax havens (*Treasure Islands*) details how finance generally—not just the offshore kind—destabilizes economies and societies globally.

Wintour, Patrick. "Tax Havens Have No Economic Justification, Say Top Economists." *Guardian*, May 9, 2016.
This article recaps and links to the open letter signed by hundreds of economists calling for the end of the offshore financial system.

CHAPTER 5: THIS SIDE OF FISCAL PARADISE

Chang, Ho-Chun Herbert, Brooke Harrington, Feng Fu, and Daniel Rockmore. "Complex Systems of Secrecy." *PNAS Nexus* 2 (2023): 1–12.
In this article, my colleagues and I offer a network analysis of big data from the Panama, Paradise, and Pandora Papers, showing that wealth managers really are the hubs of the offshore financial system—disrupt their client networks and the whole system collapses.

Cooley, Alexander, and John Heathershaw. *Dictators Without Borders: Power and Money in Central Asia.* New Haven: Yale University Press, 2019.
This book adds insight on the key role of offshore finance in supporting the power of autocrats in former Soviet socialist republics; this, in turn, is crucial to understanding the "money laundry" funding Vladimir Putin's global political strategy.

Hofri-Winogradow, Adam. "Professionals' Contribution to the Legislative Process: Between Self, Client and the Public." *Law and Social Inquiry* 39 (2014): 96–126.
This article details the Israelis' success in gaining wealth managers' cooperation to close offshore tax avoidance loopholes.

Maurer, Bill. "Complex Subjects: Offshore Finance, Complexity Theory, and the Dispersion of the Modern." *Socialist Review* 25 (1995): 114–45.
This remarkably prescient article was among the first to identify the hypermobility of the rich and their wealth as a force reconfiguring state power; Maurer's insights were essential to my own understanding of offshore finance as a more-than-economic phenomenon.

Osnos, Evan. "Doomsday Prep for the Super Rich." *New Yorker*, January 23, 2017.
This magazine article offers a deep dive into the plans of some elites to escape the collapse of society.

Rushkoff, Douglas. *Survival of the Richest: Escape Fantasies of the Tech Billionaires.* New York: W. W. Norton, 2022.
Rushkoff's account of meeting with billionaires planning their exit from society is highly relevant to many themes discussed through this book, including the motivations for elite insurgency.

INDEX

Endnotes are indicated by *n* after the page number.

Norton Shorts

BRILLIANCE WITH BREVITY

W. W. Norton & Company has been independent since 1923, when William Warder Norton and Mary (Polly) D. Herter Norton first published lectures delivered at the People's Institute, the adult education division of New York City's Cooper Union. In the 1950s, Polly Norton transferred control of the company to its employees.

One hundred years after its founding, W. W. Norton & Company inaugurates a new century of visionary independent publishing with Norton Shorts. Written by leading-edge scholars, these eye-opening books deliver bold thinking and fresh perspectives in under two hundred pages.

Available Fall 2024

Imagination: A Manifesto by Ruha Benjamin

Offshore: Stealth Wealth and the New Colonialism by Brooke Harrington

Explorers: A New History by Matthew Lockwood

Wild Girls: How the Outdoors Shaped the Women Who Challenged a Nation by Tiya Miles

Against Technoableism: Rethinking Who Needs Improvement by Ashley Shew

Literary Theory for Robots: How Computers Learned to Write by Dennis Yi Tenen

Forthcoming

Mehrsa Baradaran on the racial wealth gap

Rina Bliss on the "reality" of race

Merlin Chowkwanyun on the social determinants of health

Daniel Aldana Cohen on eco-apartheid

Jim Downs on cultural healing

Reginald K. Ellis on Black education versus Black freedom

Nicole Eustace on settler colonialism

Agustín Fuentes on human nature

Justene Hill Edwards on the history of inequality in America

Destin Jenkins on a short history of debt

Quill Kukla on a new vision of consent

Barry Lam on discretion

Kelly Lytle Hernández on the immigration regime in America

Natalia Molina on the myth of assimilation

Rhacel Salazar Parreñas on human trafficking

Tony Perry on water in African American culture and history

Beth Piatote on living with history

Ashanté Reese on the transformative possibilities of food

Jeff Sebo on the moral circle

Tracy K. Smith on poetry in an age of technology

Daniel Steinmetz-Jenkins on religion and populism

Onaje X. O. Woodbine on transcendence in sports